WINE

TASTE PAIR POUR

WINE

TASTE PAIR POUR

Grow your knowledge
with every glass

Charlotte Kristensen

MITCHELL BEAZLEY

To G, my favourite person to share a glass with, and to Izzy and Theo, for when you are old enough to join in the fun ;)

First published in Great Britain in 2024 by
Mitchell Beazley, an imprint of
Octopus Publishing Group Ltd
Carmelite House
50 Victoria Embankment
London EC4Y 0DZ
www.octopusbooks.co.uk

The authorized representative in the EEA is
Hachette Ireland, 8 Castlecourt Centre,
Dublin 15, D15 XTP3, Ireland
(email: info@hbgi.ie)

An Hachette UK Company
www.hachette.co.uk

ISBN 978-1-78472-928-8

A CIP catalogue record for this book is available
from the British Library.

Printed and bound in Slovenia

10 9 8 7 6 5 4 3 2

Publisher Alison Starling
Art Director Juliette Norsworthy
Senior Editor Alex Stetter
Editorial Assistant Ellen Sleath
Photographer Laura Jalbert
Food Stylist Natalie Thomson
Illustrator Kailee Keefe Skaberna (Kiki Makes)
Senior Production Manager Katherine Hockley

MIX
Paper | Supporting
responsible forestry
FSC® C106600

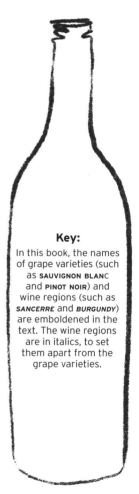

Key:
In this book, the names of grape varieties (such as SAUVIGNON BLANC and PINOT NOIR) and wine regions (such as *SANCERRE* and *BURGUNDY*) are emboldened in the text. The wine regions are in italics, to set them apart from the grape varieties.

CONTENTS

INTRODUCTION

For as long as I can remember, I've loved the ceremony of wine: selecting the wine, choosing the glassware, carefully opening the bottle, that initial sound of the first pour, the clink of the glasses – and that moment of suspense before taking a sip.

I love wine because it's about people, places and shared experiences. It can be enjoyed in many different contexts: to mark the end of a busy working day; to add a convivial touch to get-togethers with family, friends or business associates; to enhance a tasty meal; to celebrate life's special moments.

Grapes have been made into wine for several millennia. When we see a shiny bottle in a shop or restaurant it can be easy to forget that wine begins its life so humbly as fruit in a vineyard. Today wine is made in countries across the globe, from thousands of grape varieties in hundreds of styles. You could try a new wine every day for the rest of your life and barely scratch the surface.

Wine and wine people can seem a bit serious. But it's not all like that, I promise! My approach focuses on wine as a pleasurable sensory experience that's open to everyone. We can all pause for a moment and share common flavour descriptors for the wine that we're savouring – blackcurrant, violet, vanilla – and over time, we recognize patterns and take pleasure in subtle differences. Of course, wine is delicious, but it's also an absorbing interest and hobby because it's so much more than just a drink; it's inseparable from the best things in life – food, travel, culture, history and tradition.

I want to help you love wine; to discover the wines you like, how to talk about them, serve them and pair them with food. This book breaks down how to taste and describe wine, introduces key grapes and styles, has a dedicated food and wine pairing section with inspiration and recipes, and contains simple nuggets of helpful information to make buying and serving wine fun.

So grab a glass, open a bottle of something tasty and let's discover the world of wine together.

A SENSORY APPROACH TO WINE

THE LANGUAGE OF WINE

The language of wine can be confusing, esoteric and sometimes just plain bizarre. Some words seem overly technical, others seem abstract and obscure. Where's the best place to start? Is there a simple way of learning how to taste and talk about wine? And how do you build a repertoire of words to describe different wines?

Fear not! This section of the book will give you the tools to taste wine like a pro and talk confidently about the different elements of a wine. We will go through the key steps of wine tasting, explain some of the more technical language about body and texture, tannin, acidity, sweetness, alcohol and bubbles, and take a sensory approach to describing aromas, flavours and the mouthfeel of a wine.

WINE AND OUR SENSES

Wine has a magical ability to engage all our senses:

+ **Sight:** The spectrum of colours.

+ **Smell:** The range of aromas.

+ **Taste:** The variety of flavours.

+ **Touch:** The mouthfeel.

+ **Sound:** The sound of wine being poured and the stories behind the label.

Each of us has a vast library of useful sensory descriptors at our disposal when discussing wine. Our life experiences and the subjectivity of our sensory perception make for a unique and constantly evolving appreciation of every bottle.

UNTANGLING THE LANGUAGE OF WINE

One of the challenges of talking about wine is that, at its core, wine is a personal experience – we all encounter it slightly differently. There are some elements that we can make more objective statements about, for example, how sweet a wine is, as the level of sweetness can be measured. But when it comes to talking about smell and taste, things can be far more subjective. Depending on your personal preferences, what smells inviting to me might smell less so to you. Certain expressions of SAUVIGNON BLANC can display attractive garden-herb qualities to some people, but unfortunately smell like cat pee to others. Other aromas are less polarizing but we may interpret them differently, so what smells like apple to me might smell like pear to you. What reminds you of coffee, may smell more like chocolate to me. And so on...

How do we get around the issue of subjectivity and our personal experiences when it comes to aromas and flavours? Well, there's no easy fix, but the aroma and flavour wheel on pages 20–21 is a helpful starting point for categorizing some of the most common aromas and flavours found in wine, using widely understood descriptors.

> **Key:**
>
> In this book, the names of grape varieties (such as SAUVIGNON BLANC and PINOT NOIR) and wine regions (such as *SANCERRE* and *BURGUNDY*) are emboldened in the text. The wine regions are in italics, to set them apart from the grape varieties.

HOW TO TASTE WINE LIKE A PRO

There are four key steps to tasting wine like a pro. The first is to use your sense of **sight** to gather what you can from a wine's appearance. This is followed by **smell** to assess its aromas, **taste** to consider its flavours and **touch** to think about how it feels.

Sight

To assess a wine's **colour**, hold the glass at an angle over a plain surface (like a white tablecloth) so that you can see how the colour changes from the core of the wine to the rim. Natural daylight or bright lighting is best so that you can fully see the colour of the wine and its translucency.

Smell

Take an initial smell of the wine by placing your nose carefully a few centimetres from the wine. Then, give the wine a gentle swirl in the glass and smell it again to take in the **aromas**. The reason we swirl is to allow for some oxygen contact with the wine, which opens up the aromas. You may notice that different aromas pop out of the glass and become more intense after swirling.

Going through these steps might not always be feasible or appropriate in every circumstance (I get that), but it's a great idea to adopt this process when trying a wine for the first time so that you can understand your wine preferences by thinking about the different elements. With practice, you'll be able to do all these steps subtly and discreetly without making a show. But believe me, we've all had our fair share of swirling spills in our time.

Taste
Take a sip and work the wine around your mouth. Almost chew it and draw in a little air for added oxygen contact to release all the **flavours** in your mouth. Consider the flavours at the beginning and on the finish, and whether the sensation is more drying or sweet.

Touch
By working the wine around your mouth you will appreciate its **mouthfeel** and get a sense of its body and texture, tannin, acidity, alcohol and bubbles.

Let's dive into each of these steps further...

SIGHT

Engaging our sight adds to the full experience of wine tasting. Just as we eat first with our eyes, we drink first with our eyes too – we are attracted to certain colours and tones.

Beyond the obvious (white, red or rosé, still or sparkling), we can tell a lot about a wine from just the way it looks:

+ Colour and age of the wine: Many young white wines are light-to-medium yellow in colour and, as they age, they may become a richer yellow or golden colour. Young red wines are often a light-to-deep red colour (some may even have a purple tinge) and as they age, they may become a brick-like or reddish-brown colour.

+ Colour and grape variety: Certain grape varieties can produce wines with distinctive colours. Thin-skinned red varieties, such as GRENACHE and PINOT NOIR, typically produce lighter-coloured and more translucent wines, whereas thick-skinned varieties, such as CABERNET SAUVIGNON and SYRAH (often known as SHIRAZ in the New World), produce deeper-coloured and more opaque wines. MALBEC is known for producing distinctive purple-hued wines and thin-skinned NEBBIOLO commonly turns a garnet colour after just a few years in the bottle.

+ Colour and style of wine: Oaked, full-bodied white wines often have a deeper colour than unoaked, light wines. Sweet white wines can vary from pale yellow through to a deep-golden amber colour. Lighter-coloured, translucent red wines often indicate that the style is lighter-bodied and lower in alcohol – but note there are exceptions, such as NEBBIOLO and GRENACHE, which may give you a surprise. Deep-coloured reds may indicate a fuller-bodied, higher alcohol wine, such as CABERNET SAUVIGNON.

Wine Doctor

HELP! Is my wine OK?

Q My wine is brown. Does that mean it is past its best?

That depends on the wine. Some wines are meant to be brown, including some fortified wines, such as certain styles of sherry and tawny port. But for the majority of wines, a brown colour indicates that the wine is oxidized – a series of chemical reactions have occurred as a result of the wine coming into contact with air. So if you find a bottle of PINOT GRIGIO or SAUVIGNON BLANC with a brown tinge at the back of your cupboard, then I'm afraid it's time to say goodbye and pour that down the sink. Some red wines that are meant for long-term ageing, such as quality wines from BORDEAUX or BAROLO, will develop a garnet hue over time, but once a wine has turned a dominant brown colour it's likely to indicate the wine is past its best.

Q My wine is hazy. What's wrong with it?

Most wines will be free from any haziness thanks to fining and filtration practices in the winery. Fining seeks to remove large unwanted particles that could negatively affect the aromas and flavours of the wine, while filtration further clarifies the wine so it's an appealing, clear liquid. However, some winemakers believe that overly fining and filtering a wine removes some of its character, so they may choose not to employ these practices, or apply them only lightly. As a result, their wines might have a slightly cloudy or hazy appearance, which tends to be more noticeable in white or rosé wines, given their translucency. Many good-quality through to fine wines are made like this, so haziness doesn't necessarily indicate a problem with a wine.

Q My wine has tiny crystals in it. What are they?

Keep calm! The little crystals you may notice on a cork or at the bottom of the wine bottle are tartrates, a completely natural by-product of wine as it ages. Known affectionately as 'wine diamonds', they are commonplace and do not emit aromas or flavours. Some winemakers choose to force these crystals to develop earlier in the winemaking process so that they can remove them before bottling. However, many winemakers choose not to do this. The crystals will not harm the wine, so you can gently reassure your guests if there is any commotion.

Q My wine has sediment in it. Can I still drink it?

Like wine crystals, sediment in wine is a normal and natural by-product, but it does have a grainy and gritty texture that can make the wine unpleasant to drink – a bit like coffee granules that have escaped the filter, which is never a pleasant experience. If you have a wine with a lot of sediment, you can use a decanter to help separate it from the wine (see page 183), or otherwise just be careful not to pour out the end of the bottle, as it contains most of the sediment.

SMELL AND TASTE

Smell and taste are the primary senses engaged in drinking wine. Some aromas and flavours may remind you of fruit, herbs and flowers, but they may also be evocative of places, people and occasions, as wine has a special way of unlocking memories and experiences. The range and complexity of aromas and flavours found in a glass of wine are what elevate it from a simple alcoholic beverage to a unique and charming sensory experience.

Physiologically, smell and taste are two different senses, but they are linked. Don't underestimate the power of your nose when it comes to tasting wine. It often takes the lead in anticipating how something will taste – and of course a blocked nose can have a disastrous impact on your taste perception of wine in the same way that it can for your food.

Try this: Next time you have a glass in front of you, take a sip, then another sip while holding your nose. You'll notice when you hold your nose that the flavours don't seem as powerful. This is because when you taste food or wine, olfactory receptors in your nose send messages to your brain at the same time as receptors on your tongue. The receptors in the nose intensify the tasting experience, so if these are blocked, a wine's flavours will seem muted.

WHY DO WE SMELL WINE BEFORE TASTING IT?

The primary purpose of smelling a wine after it's been poured (and before tasting it) is to check whether there are any defects or problems with the wine, most of which we can detect with our nose without even needing to take a sip. Some of the smells that indicate an issue are:

+ wet cardboard, mustiness (corked or cork taint).
+ vinegar (oxidized).
+ stale fruit or lacking in fruit (oxidized).
+ nutty and cooked fruit (oxidized or damaged from heat exposure).
+ any other potent unattractive smell.

Where it can get a bit tricky is that certain aromas can smell off-putting to some individuals, but this may be a personal preference as opposed to indicating a problem with the wine. Some unusual smells may be deliberate stylistic choices made by the winemaker that some people have greater sensitivity to than others. Some of these less appetizing aromas might blow off after a wine has been opened and exposed to oxygen for a short while. At other times, unappealing aromas may stick around and suggest a problem with the wine, or that it's not to your liking. Some of the more ambiguous aromas can smell of eggs, varnish, animals, stewed fruit, a struck match or a dominant nuttiness.

If you're in a restaurant or bar and unsure if there is a problem with your wine, check with your waiter or sommelier. If you've purchased a wine from a specialist wine shop, contact them and ask for advice. In other circumstances, if the wine isn't to your liking, don't force yourself to drink it – after all, wine should be a pleasurable experience.

Aroma and flavour wheel

There are many categories of aromas and flavours that can be appreciated in wine, which can broadly be attributed to:

+ the particular grape variety.
+ the fermentation process.
+ the type of vessel used in winemaking (an oak barrel, for example) and other winemaking techniques.
+ ageing the wine.

The aroma and flavour wheel displays many of the typical aromas and flavours found in wine, using examples that are widely recognized and easily understood, making it a great starting point for describing a wine to others.

Generally, more simple wines will have aromas and flavours from one or a couple of the categories. More complex wines will span several different categories in the wheel, and the flavours will persist on the palate for longer, which is referred to as a 'long finish'.

Stewed/dried fruit
raisin, prune, jammy, cooked fruit, dried fruit

Earth
meat, leather, mushroom, savoury, forest, hay, coffee, tea

Smoke
tobacco, tar, graphite, kerosene

Wood
toasty, cedar, clove, vanilla, cinnamon

Spice
white pepper, black pepper, ginger, aromatic spice

Bread
pastry, brioche

Dairy
buttery, creamy, yogurt

Nutty
coconut, almond, walnut, hazelnut

Sweet
honey, caramel, cocoa

Green fruit
apple, pear, gooseberry

Citrus fruit
lemon, lime, grapefruit, orange

Stone fruit
peach, nectarine, apricot

Red fruit
strawberry, raspberry, red cherry, cranberry

Black fruit
blackcurrant, black cherry, blackberry, blueberry, plum

Tropical fruit
mango, pineapple, lychee, melon, banana, passion fruit

Mineral
wet stone, saline, chalk, flint, slate, iron, gravel

Botanical
stalky, herb, grass, medicinal, eucalyptus, leafy

Floral
jasmine, honeysuckle, blossom, violet, rose

Winemaking vessels and techniques can contribute to aromas and flavours in the nutty, spice, wood, dairy and bread categories.

With age, a wine can develop aromas and flavours in the sweet, nutty, smoke, earth and stewed/dried fruit categories.

Aromas and flavours

Q What is a dry wine?
When it comes to wine, dry is the opposite of sweet – it means there is no sugar, or only a tiny amount, present in the wine. The naturally present sugars in the grape will have been converted into alcohol and carbon dioxide during the fermentation process (see page 34 for more about this). Wines can be made at all sorts of sweetness levels, from what is described as bone dry (very dry) all the way through to lusciously sweet (see page 26 for more detail).

Q What is a sweet wine?
Have you ever smelled a white wine bursting with fruit aromas and then taken a sip only to notice that it doesn't leave a sweet taste in your mouth? This is in essence the difference between a fruity wine as opposed to a sweet wine. A fruity wine displays well-defined fruit flavours on the nose and palate but doesn't have any (or only a small amount of) sugar actually present in the wine. The best way of detecting whether a wine is dry or sweet is by thinking about the finish – is the lasting sensation more drying or is it sweet? I often use the analogy of fruit teas when thinking about this. For example, strawberry tea triggers your brain into thinking you're about to try something sweet, but when you take a sip, it has all the flavour of strawberry, but none of the sweetness on the finish.

Q What happens to aromas and flavours as a wine ages?
Most wines are intended to be drunk within a year or two of being made. After this time, they begin to lose their aromas, flavours and freshness and start to taste muted and stale. A small number of wines benefit from ageing, their character positively evolving over time. Looking at the flavour wheel on pages 20–1, some of the attractive and complex aromas and flavours that can develop through ageing are those in the sweet, nutty, smoke, earth and stewed/dried fruit categories. A wine's texture can develop positively through the ageing process; wines with high levels of tannin and acidity will soften over time and become better integrated with the flavours on the palate for an overall more balanced feel.

BUILDING YOUR WINE VOCABULARY

Before I took my first wine-tasting exam, my tutor suggested in the weeks prior to the assessment that I should practise tasting wine with a buddy and make an effort every day to acknowledge the aromas and flavours I encountered to expand my sensory library of descriptors. Now, I'm not suggesting you need to be part of a wine-tasting group or begin a smelling or tasting expedition to enjoy wine as a hobby. But talking to others and being aware of the different aromas and flavours that crop up in everyday life are simple ways of building your wine vocabulary and sensory library.

TWO PALATES ARE BETTER THAN ONE

I've found tasting wine with another person or in a group fun, sociable and a brilliant way of learning more about different wines. There have been many occasions where a specific aroma or flavour has been on the tip of my tongue, but I haven't quite worked out what it is – step in my tasting partner or group, who have helped me work it out. Hearing other people's suggestions can help you find words to describe your own experience and can also give you someone else's perspective on aromas and flavours that you may not have considered, so broadening your overall tasting experience.

AROMAS AND FLAVOURS IN EVERYDAY LIFE

We encounter many different objects, places and foods in daily life that can help us build our repertoire of words to describe wine. When opportunities arise naturally, such as when making coffee, baking a cake or buying fruit and vegetables, take a moment to appreciate those items. You'll begin to be more aware of subtle aromatic nuances, such as those between lemon and lime, coconut and vanilla, or clove and cinnamon. And you'll be surprised by how many of these items you'll begin to pick out in your wines as you add to your aroma and flavour memory bank.

TOUCH

When we taste wine, not only do we appreciate its flavours but also how it feels. Let's look further at the key sensations we feel on our palate: body and texture, tannin, acidity, sweetness, alcohol and bubbles.

BODY AND TEXTURE

Body is the weight of a wine and texture is the sensation of the wine. Light-bodied wines have a consistency closer to water, whereas full-bodied wines have more weight, like full-fat milk. Medium-bodied wines sit at varying levels in between those bookends. Lighter-bodied wines tend to be easier to drink, whereas fuller-bodied wines have a more ample consistency, so tend to be drunk more slowly. So, when considering the body of a wine, think about both how heavy it feels in your mouth and how easy it is to drink. Wines with higher levels of alcohol will often be fuller-bodied than those with lower levels of alcohol, as will wines with higher levels of sugar compared to their lower-sugar counterparts (but note there are some exceptions). Oak use during winemaking can also contribute to the weight of a wine and its tannin content (see opposite). Tannin provides texture to a wine, but winemaking techniques, such as malolactic conversion and lees ageing, can also add to texture (see pages 42–3).

+ **Grapes with a light body:** White grape PINOT GRIGIO and red grape PINOT NOIR.
+ **Grapes with a medium body:** White grape SAUVIGNON BLANC and red grape CABERNET FRANC.
+ **Grapes with a full body:** White grape CHARDONNAY (oaked) and red grape CABERNET SAUVIGNON.

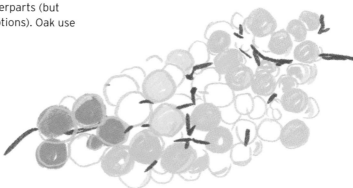

TANNIN

Tannin contributes a drying and gripping sensation – it has a bitterness that feels a bit mouth-puckering, like drinking a very strong cup of black tea. Tannin comes from the skins of the grape, so in most cases we only refer to tannin in red wines, as white winemaking uses only the pulp of a grape. Some red wines (for example, certain styles of CABERNET SAUVIGNON) can be very tannic in their youth, but the tannins will soften over time, which is one of the reasons why some wines benefit from ageing. The texture of tannins will depend on the grape variety and other factors, such as where the wine is grown, how it is made or the vintage (note that oak use in winemaking can also contribute to tannin). When thinking about the nature of the tannins, consider whether they feel light and silky, smooth and velvety, fine and firm, or powerful and gripping. We all have different tolerances and preferences – some people like the feel of a grippy tannic wine, whereas others prefer light and silky tannins; or, if you're like me, it depends on the time, occasion and what I am eating. High-tannin wines work especially well with meat dishes, as they bind to proteins and fat, which soften them.

+ **Red grapes with low tannins:** PINOT NOIR and GAMAY.
+ **Red grapes with medium tannins:** MERLOT and GRENACHE.
+ **Red grapes with high tannins:** NEBBIOLO and CABERNET SAUVIGNON.

ACIDITY

Acid is found in a grape's pulp and is essential for producing wines that taste well-balanced. A wine can feel flat and lacklustre if there is not enough acidity to keep the flavours feeling fresh. Acidity is especially important in sweet wines as it balances the high sugar content, without which a sweet wine would feel cloying and flabby (that 'meh' sensation on the palate). Acidity in wine naturally makes our mouth water after we have taken a sip, so even though we may not notice the acidity in some wines, our salivary glands will be the giveaway. Acidity is important in red wines, too, for balance, and is also a key attribute for helping a wine to age, as it has preservative qualities.

+ **Grapes with lower levels of acidity:** White grape VIOGNIER and red grape GRENACHE.
+ **Grapes with higher levels of acidity:** White grapes RIESLING and SAUVIGNON BLANC and red grapes PINOT NOIR and SANGIOVESE.

SWEETNESS

Sweetness is the amount of sugar in a wine and it is best detected in the finish. Sweetness is closely related to aroma and flavour (see pages 20–3) and to the body of a wine (see page 24). At one end of the spectrum, we have bone-dry wines with no detectable sweetness, and at the other end, we have very sweet wines with extremely high levels of sugar. Like tannin and acidity, high levels of sugar can also help a wine to age. We sense sweetness most notably on the tip of our tongue.

+ **Bone dry:** No detectable sweetness.
+ **Dry:** Little-to-no detectable sweetness.
+ **Off-dry:** A small amount of sweetness.
+ **Medium-dry to medium-sweet:** Discernible sweetness.
+ **Sweet:** Distinctive sweetness.
+ **Lusciously sweet:** Extremely high levels of sweetness.

Q What is a structured wine? This term is generally used to describe a wine that has high levels of tannin (mostly for red wines) and high levels of acidity along with a great depth of concentration of flavours. These components are key to giving a wine the potential to age. See more about ageing on page 22.

ALCOHOL

Alcohol is produced during fermentation and gives a warming sensation on our palates. It is measured as alcohol-by-volume (ABV) and is presented as a percentage on the label of a bottle. Well-made wines seek to integrate alcohol seamlessly, to avoid that burn and so that it isn't a defining characteristic. Most still wines sit within 10–15% ABV but there are some examples lower and higher than this typical range. Fortified wines (see page 66) have alcohol added to them and are usually within 15–22% ABV.

BUBBLES

Bubbles in wine are created by carbon dioxide and we sense them all over our mouth. The force and texture of bubbles will depend on the method in which they are made, as well as storage conditions, age of the wine and for how long a bottle has been open. When tasting a wine with bubbles, consider the nature of the bubbles: is there a gentle spritz, are they foamy and frothy, or fine and persistent? See more about sparkling wines on pages 59–63.

SOUND

To complete our sensory appreciation of wine, let's take a moment to consider how our sense of sound is engaged when drinking wine.

Many actions involved in wine are aural and will stimulate other senses in anticipation: from the celebratory 'pop' of champagne to the subtle 'phut' of a cork releasing; from the harmonious 'glug, glug, glug' of a wine pour to the gentle (and sometimes not so gentle!) 'clink' of glasses raised in a toast.

We also have the sound of the stories behind a wine - the place in which it is made, the history of that spot, the uniqueness of the land, the inspiration behind the bottles and the people who made it. These tales can elevate the whole experience of drinking wine.

PUTTING IT ALL TOGETHER

Let's think about how we can describe a wine by working through the four wine-tasting steps we have covered in this chapter and the questions they raise regarding sight, smell, taste and touch.

SIGHT

+ Is the wine white, red, rosé, orange or brown?
+ Is it still or does it have bubbles?
+ Is the colour faint or is it rich?
+ Is the wine light and translucent in colour, a medium depth, or a deep opaque?
+ Is there anything else you notice about the wine – is it hazy, are there crystals or traces of sediment?

SMELL

Look at the aroma and flavour wheel on pages 20–1 for a breakdown of categories.

+ Does the wine smell fruity?
+ For white wine – are the fruit flavours of fresh fruit? Are they of green and citrus fruit (less ripe), or stone and tropical fruit (riper)?
+ For red wine – are the fruit flavours of fresh fruit? If so, are they tart or ripe? Are the fruit flavours of red fruit or black fruit, or a mixture of both?
+ Does the wine display any dried or stewed fruit flavours, which may indicate that it has started to evolve with age?
+ Does the wine display any green, mineral, floral or sweet aromas?
+ Are there any dairy or bread aromas, which may indicate winemaking techniques (lees or malolactic conversion)?
+ Are there any spice or wood aromas, which may indicate winemaking techniques (oak)?
+ Are there any smoke or earth aromas, which may indicate that the wine has started to evolve with age?

TASTE

+ Do the flavours you taste match the aromas you smell?
+ Is the wine drying on the finish or do you notice any sweetness? If the latter, at what level?
+ Does the wine have a long finish?

TOUCH

+ Body and texture – does the weight feel light, medium or heavy? Is it easy to drink or does it have a fuller consistency for slower sipping? Does the texture feel creamy or buttery? If the wine is sweet, is this giving it weight?
+ Tannins for red wine – do you notice a drying or gripping sensation? How intense is this sensation? Do the tannins feel light and silky, smooth and velvety, fine and firm, or powerful and gripping?
+ Acidity – does your mouth water after you've taken a sip? Is this intense, indicating high acidity, or less so?
+ Alcohol – do you notice a warming sensation? Is this well integrated?
+ Bubbles – does the wine have bubbles? A gentle spritz, foamy and frothy, or fine and persistent?

DO YOU LIKE IT?

The most important question is here at the end. Do you like the wine? What do you like about it? Think about colour, aromas, taste and touch. And, of course, although this is not part of many formal tasting notes, think about how the aural aspects of the experience – the cork popping, the gentle fizz of delicate bubbles in your glass, the winemaker's story and history – enhance your appreciation of the wine.

CRAFTING A WINE-TASTING NOTE

Let's put things into practice by looking at two different wines and crafting tasting notes for each one. We'll start with a short, subjective description of the wine that sets the scene – the type of tasting note you could find on the back of a wine bottle or in a restaurant wine list. Then we'll go through the key tasting steps to break down specific features and put together a more objective description of the wine to give a full sensory picture.

RED WINE: NAPA VALLEY CABERNET SAUVIGNON

This is a tasting note for a classic oaked style of CABERNET SAUVIGNON from California's NAPA VALLEY, with a few years of bottle age.

Sensory description:
It's a bold red wine with a powerful structure – mouth-hugging and opulent with layers of black fruit, old-cigar-box notes and evocative of a forest walk.

Key tasting steps:

SIGHT It's a still red wine with a deep, opaque ruby colour.

SMELL It has fresh and ripe black fruit aromas of blackberry and blackcurrant; wood aromas of clove and a hint of vanilla, some smoke aromas of tobacco and earthy coffee aromas.

TASTE The wine is dry and the flavours are similar to the aromas. The finish is long.

TOUCH The wine is full-bodied as it feels heavy in the mouth and has a fuller consistency for slower sipping. The tannins are noticeably high and feel powerful but smooth. The level of acidity is high, indicated by how much it makes the mouth water on the finish. There is a noticeable warmth, indicating a high level of alcohol, but it feels balanced with the other elements of the wine.

WHITE WINE: SANCERRE SAUVIGNON BLANC

This is a tasting note for a classic, youthful unoaked style of SAUVIGNON BLANC from SANCERRE in the LOIRE VALLEY, France.

Sensory description:
It's a fresh and elegant white wine, evocative of an apple orchard and herb garden; it has refreshing citrus notes and is reminiscent of a bright rainy afternoon in the mountains.

Key tasting steps:

SIGHT It's a still white wine with a bright pale-lemon colour.

SMELL It has fresh aromas of green fruit – apple, pear and gooseberry – and some citrusy lemon aromas. Also subtle green aromas of grass and herbs, and mineral aromas of wet stone and flint.

TASTE The wine is dry and the flavours are similar to the aromas. The finish is long.

TOUCH It is light-bodied, feels light in weight and is easy to sip. The wine has a high level of acidity, indicated by how much it makes the mouth water on the finish. The alcohol is not noticeable and seems well-integrated into the wine, indicating that it isn't high in alcohol.

PLACES, PEOPLE AND PRODUCTION

A SHORT HISTORY OF WINEMAKING

In simple terms, wine is made from fermented grapes. Most grapes used in the production of wine are from the vine species *Vitis vinifera*, which includes famous varieties such as CHARDONNAY and MERLOT, as well as less well-known and rare varieties. Grapes used for winemaking are planted widely across the world, but most wine production takes place in only a few dozen countries.

ANATOMY OF A GRAPE

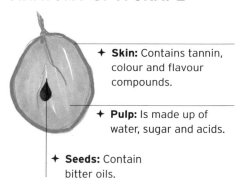

+ Skin: Contains tannin, colour and flavour compounds.

+ Pulp: Is made up of water, sugar and acids.

+ Seeds: Contain bitter oils.

FERMENTATION

Wine production is believed to date back to around 6000 BCE, when very basic equipment was used. Two essential elements are required for alcoholic fermentation: sugar and yeast. Early production of wine relied on simple vessels for winemaking, such as large clay pots. Alcoholic fermentation would take place by the yeasts that naturally exist on the grape skins and in the atmosphere, converting the sugars found in the pulp of the grape into wine. In modern winemaking various vessels are available, yeasts may be added to assist fermentation, and a host of different machinery and technology can aid many processes from start to finish – including harvesting grapes, crushing and pressing grapes, controlling the temperature of fermentation and bottling the wine.

**Formula for alcoholic fermentation:
sugar + yeast = alcohol + carbon dioxide**

THE LIFE OF A VINE

It can take several years for a vine to start bearing fruit suitable for wine production. So if you're dreaming of planting your own vineyard one day, remember you're in it for the long run! Once productive, most vines bear fruit annually for around 25–30 years, but some vines will produce quality fruit for 50 years or more. You may have seen the term 'old vines', or the French *vieilles vignes* (or similar translation), on a bottle label. Although there is not a legal definition of old vines, the term is generally used to recognize vines over 35 years of age. These mature vines are low-yielding, but produce wines with concentrated fruit, purity and complexity.

30-50 DEGREES LATITUDE

Historically, wine regions have sat within two bands of latitude around the Earth, approximately 30-50 degrees north and 30-50 degrees south. The northern band includes large parts of Europe, the Middle East, North Africa, the USA and China. The southern band includes New Zealand and parts of Chile, Argentina, South Africa and Australia.

However, today wine is being made outside these latitudes in countries that were previously considered unable to produce reliable harvests and quality wines. For instance, wines are being made in the UK (previously considered too cold and wet) and in countries such as India and Mexico (previously considered too hot or humid). Producers in these marginal regions often plant vineyards at very specific site locations that have favourable conditions, carefully select grape varieties that cope well in the particular climate, and use technology and know-how to aid the production of quality wines.

OLD WORLD VS. NEW WORLD

You may have heard of 'Old World' and 'New World' wines and wondered what these terms mean. Old World refers to countries where vines for winemaking originated, and covers Europe, the Middle East and northern Africa. New World refers to countries where vines for winemaking were imported, and this includes major wine regions, such as the USA, China, Chile, Argentina, South Africa and Australia.

Historically, there was a noticeable stylistic difference between Old and New World wines. Old World regions tended to have cooler climates, leading to subtly fruity wines with a lighter body, higher acidity and lower alcohol – often referred to as restrained in style. New World regions tended to have warmer climates, leading to riper, fruitier wines with a fuller body, lower levels of acidity and more alcohol – often referred to as bold in style. Today the differences in style between the two regions are not as clear-cut. Many New World producers seek out cool sites and employ techniques to make more restrained and lighter Old World styles, and many producers in warm areas of southern Europe make ripe and full-bodied New World-style wines.

HOW PLACE AFFECTS GRAPES

If you've ever turned your hand to a spot of gardening, you may have noticed how different conditions affect the quality of your crop. A heatwave may have given you trophy-worthy extra-sweet strawberries one year, whereas extended downpours and cool temperatures may have caused disappointingly soggy and rotten lettuces another year. Grapes, like other types of fruit and vegetable, are affected by the place in which they are grown and the conditions for that year, which is known as the vintage. Certain grapes thrive in warm climates, whereas other varieties are better suited to cool climates. Some grapes, such as CHARDONNAY, can be grown in both cool and warm climates, though the style of the resulting wine may vary greatly (see page 72 for more on this grape).

The intricacies of how a place affects the vine is beyond the scope of this book, but some of the key factors are introduced here: climate, weather, aspect and altitude, and soil.

CLIMATE

Warm climate or cool climate

Broadly speaking, wine regions in warm climates produce wines with bold and ripe aromas and flavours, a full body, lower levels of acidity, high alcohol, plus high and powerful tannins (for red wines). By contrast, wine regions in cooler climates produce wines that have more subtle and less ripe aromas and flavours, with a lighter body, higher levels of acidity, low alcohol, plus medium and grippy tannins (for red wines).

+ **Examples of warm regions:** NAPA VALLEY in California, BAROSSA VALLEY in Australia, PUGLIA in Italy.
+ **Examples of cool regions:** MOSEL in Germany, CHABLIS in France, the whole of England.

WEATHER

Weather variation from year to year (that is to say, from vintage to vintage)

Some wine regions experience more variable weather from year to year (known as vintage variation) than other regions with more predictable weather. This is why the vintage is very important for certain regions and less so for others. For example, BORDEAUX and CHAMPAGNE in France can have extremely variable weather from year to year, with some years producing markedly better-quality grapes than others.

ASPECT AND ALTITUDE

The direction in which the vineyards face and the altitude at which they are planted

South- and west-facing vineyards in the northern hemisphere and north- and west-facing vineyards in the southern hemisphere generally experience more sun and warmth, leading to riper styles of wine. Conversely, north- and east-facing vineyards in the northern hemisphere and south- and east-facing vineyards in the southern hemisphere generally experience less sun and warmth, leading to less ripe styles of wines. High-altitude sites are generally cooler and temperatures fluctuate more significantly between day and night, which can slow the ripening process and help grapes retain fresh flavours and acidity.

SOIL

The type of soil in which vines grow

The consistency and type of soil in which a vine is planted can affect the aromas, flavours and feel of a wine. Generally, the best grapes for wine are grown in poorer, free-draining soils. These conditions force a vine to focus its efforts on producing fruit, instead of growing shoots and leaves, and the reduced availability of water leads to more concentrated flavours and sugars (less dilution). Some common soil types in wine regions include sand, limestone, clay and volcanic.

Terroir

The French word *terroir* is used to refer to the uniqueness of an individual place in which a vine is grown and how that affects the resulting wine. Terroir-driven wines seek to capture the place they are from, and those who appreciate these wines value the nuances in the aromas, flavours and feel of a wine influenced by a particular place. Some grapes are considered particularly terroir-reflective in taking on the identity of a place, such as the red grapes PINOT NOIR and NEBBIOLO, and the white grapes CHARDONNAY and RIESLING.

HOW WINE IS MADE

Let's move on to the key steps in winemaking. Harvest is a busy time in the wine calendar, and once the grapes are brought into the winery, there are a number of choices a winemaker can make that affect the style of the wine. Here is a summary of the key steps in white and red winemaking from harvest to bottling.

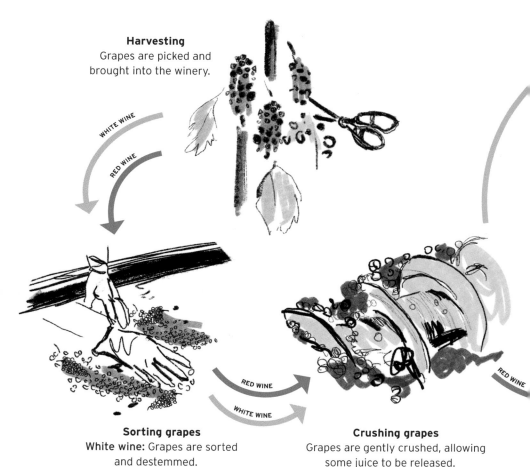

Harvesting
Grapes are picked and brought into the winery.

WHITE WINE

RED WINE

RED WINE

WHITE WINE

RED WINE

Sorting grapes
White wine: Grapes are sorted and destemmed.
Red wine: Grapes are sorted and may or may not be destemmed.

Crushing grapes
Grapes are gently crushed, allowing some juice to be released.

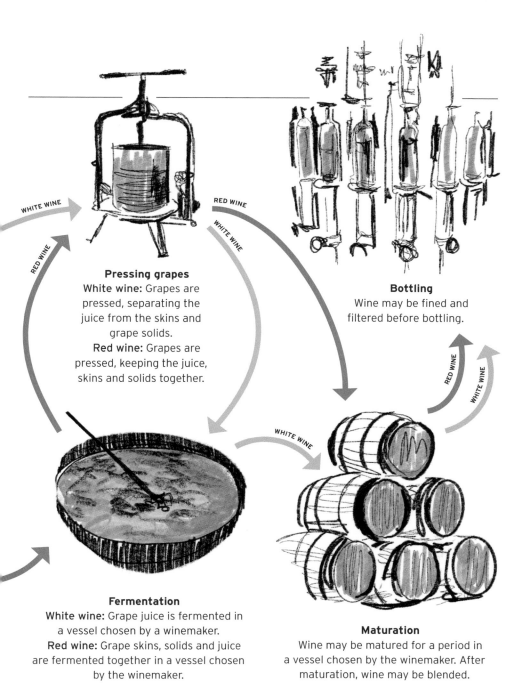

Pressing grapes
White wine: Grapes are pressed, separating the juice from the skins and grape solids.
Red wine: Grapes are pressed, keeping the juice, skins and solids together.

Bottling
Wine may be fined and filtered before bottling.

Fermentation
White wine: Grape juice is fermented in a vessel chosen by a winemaker.
Red wine: Grape skins, solids and juice are fermented together in a vessel chosen by the winemaker.

Maturation
Wine may be matured for a period in a vessel chosen by the winemaker. After maturation, wine may be blended.

WHITE WINE
RED WINE
RED WINE
WHITE WINE
RED WINE
WHITE WINE
WHITE WINE

HOW WINEMAKING TECHNIQUES AFFECT THE TASTE OF WINE

A winemaker may employ a number of different processes and techniques during the winemaking process: some can have a big impact on the resulting wine while others provide more nuanced features. Let's have a look at some of the key winemaking techniques that affect the aromas, flavours and feel of a wine.

Vessels are containers used for fermenting and maturing wine. They are most commonly made from oak or stainless steel, but vessels can take many shapes and forms, from ancient-style clay amphorae to concrete eggs, and can be made from plastic, glass and different types of wood. So, how do vessels affect wine?

Oak can add cedar, toasty and vanilla aromas and flavours to wine (see 'wood' in the aroma and flavour wheel on page 20 for more common descriptors). The intensity of these aromas and flavours are affected by the type of oak used (most common are French oak and American oak), how the barrel is made, its size and whether it has been used in winemaking in previous vintages. The first time an oak barrel is used, it's known as a 'new oak' barrel. New oak barrels become 'neutral' after about three vintages of holding wine, but they can still be used as the oak will allow gentle oxygen transfer through the wood and bunghole, which enhances

certain wines. Oak barrels can also contribute towards the tannin in a wine.

Stainless steel is used to preserve a wine's fresh and fruity qualities – it's an inert material, so a stainless steel vessel doesn't impart aromas or flavours to the wine. It's also non-porous, so doesn't allow oxygen transfer. (Preventing oxygen contact during the winemaking process is desirable for certain grapes and/or styles.)

Blending is a specialist skill that usually takes place after the maturation process. The art of blending can take a lifetime to master, with many producers passing down family secrets for generations. Some producers blend grapes of the same variety from different vineyards that may display slightly different characteristics to achieve a desired final wine. Wines made from one variety are often referred to as 'varietal wines'. Other producers grow several different grape varieties and choose to blend them all together, bringing a range of attributes to the final wine – see more on CHAMPAGNE (page 61), BORDEAUX (page 205) and GRENACHE-SYRAH-MOURVÈDRE (or GSM) blends (page 94).

Malolactic conversion is a process that may occur naturally after fermentation, or be induced by the winemaker, usually resulting in buttery, creamy notes and a rounder texture to a wine. You may have come across CHARDONNAY described as 'buttery', which is likely to have undergone this process. Some winemakers may choose

to avoid it to retain a wine's freshness and vibrancy – for example, some *SANCERRE SAUVIGNON BLANC* producers choose to restrict malolactic conversion (see more on this wine on page 70).

Lees ageing involves the use of yeasts after they have done their job during fermentation and died. The dead yeast cells, known as 'lees', don't necessarily become redundant: some winemakers choose to keep their wines in contact with them, which can add notes of biscuits and brioche and a richer, creamier texture to the wine. See, for example, *CHAMPAGNE* (page 61) and *MUSCADET* (page 86).

DIFFERENT WINE-GROWING AND WINEMAKING PRACTICES

The terms organic, biodynamic and natural have become buzzwords in the wine world. However, these words are often misunderstood and used interchangeably, creating confusion. These approaches focus on practices in the vineyard and in the winery; they are different, but do involve some overlapping features, which are outlined below. Before delving into the topic further, let's have a look at how organic, biodynamic and natural approaches differ from conventional winemaking.

Conventional winemaking includes many popular wines that we find at all quality and price levels. Certain chemical products can be used in the vineyard to tackle issues, such as wet weather, pests and fungal diseases, in order to aid consistent and plentiful harvests. Products may also be used in the winery to adjust elements of a wine, such as the levels of alcohol, sugar and tannin, and to clarify, stabilize and preserve a wine.

Organic winemaking generally prohibits the use of chemical products and advocates for natural products and agricultural diversity to create healthy vineyards. Producers may apply for organic certification, which is shown on the label of a bottle. Some producers may follow organic practices but not apply for certification for reasons of time or cost, among others. There are also a number of other sustainable certifications available, which are typically shown on the label of a bottle.

Biodynamic winemakers adopt organic practices but go a step further, taking a holistic, ecological and ethical approach towards farming, looking at the life of the vineyard as a whole ecosystem. Using the lunar calendar and other astronomical events as guidance, they embrace spiritual practices and preparations. The biodynamic federation Demeter certifies producers around the world.

Natural wines are made from organically farmed grapes (some may also be biodynamic), but the key difference is the focus on practices employed in the winery. Producers embrace a hands-off approach that is often referred to as minimal- or low-intervention winemaking. For many of them, the goal is to produce wines that are hand-crafted, characterful and reflective of their terroir (see page 39) without using the methods for intervention and adjustment that are common in conventional winemaking and which are thought to conceal terroir. Key features of this approach include using wild or native yeasts (that naturally exist on the grape or in the atmosphere), not using additives or over-intrusive machinery, using vessels that have minimal impact on the flavour of the wine, undertaking limited or no filtering or fining, and making limited or no use of sulphur (there is some dispute about this). The word 'natural' is controversial in the wine world, suggesting as it does that other wines are not natural. Producers across the world have long practised these approaches but choose not to call themselves natural winemakers. Many of the techniques used to make natural wines are not new and, if anything, go back to earlier winemaking practices before the involvement of chemicals, technology and machinery. In 2020, a new body was launched in France recognizing this approach with a new certification logo, Vin Méthode Nature, which has since expanded outside France into other European countries.

The big sulphur debate

There's lots of noise about the use of sulphur dioxide in winemaking, how it affects a wine and whether it causes headaches and allergies, so let's look at the key questions.

Q Why is there sulphur dioxide in wine?

Sulphur dioxide is produced naturally during the wine fermentation process, but it may also be added by a winemaker to control several issues that arise throughout the wine production process, from the point of harvest until bottling.

Q What's the key benefit of sulphur dioxide in wine?

Sulphur dioxide is an antioxidant and antibacterial agent that helps preserve wine and keep it smelling and tasting fresh.

Q What's the key disadvantage of adding sulphur dioxide to wine?

Overuse of sulphur dioxide causes a wine to lose its character by dulling aromas and flavours.

Q Am I allergic to sulphur dioxide, as I get a headache when I drink wines with sulphites?

For most people, it's unlikely that sulphites are causing your headaches – the use of sulphur dioxide is highly regulated around the world and it is far more likely that headaches are caused by overconsumption and dehydration. Comparatively few people are allergic to sulphites, and for those who are, the adverse reaction is usually asthmatic symptoms. Sulphites are a commonly used preservative in many other types of food and drink, such as dried fruit, biscuits and sauces.

Winemaking – where science meets art

Winemakers may use machinery and equipment to monitor the progress of a wine throughout the production process. Additionally, they may regularly sample their wine to assess its development. The human tools of sight, smell, taste and touch, plus experience gained from past vintages, are invaluable for making key decisions along the winemaking journey.

STYLES
AND
GRAPES

RED WINE

Red wines can range from silky and fragrant to bold and powerful, from *glou-glou* in style (I love this French term for young and quaffable reds) to aged, gastronomic and thought-provoking. They can be enjoyed in a cosy setting by the fire on a frosty evening or served lightly chilled on a warm and balmy afternoon.

When making red wine, both the skin and the pulp of red grapes are used. Red wines get their colour and tannin from the grape skin. They can range in colour from a light and translucent vibrant crimson to a deep, dark red, and can become a brick-like or reddish-brown colour with age.

KEY STYLES OF RED WINE

Grapes producing light-bodied and fruity red wines with silky tannins:
PINOT NOIR (page 88)
GAMAY (page 108)
FRAPPATO (page 112)

Grapes producing medium-to-full-bodied red wines with juicy fruit and velvety tannins:
MERLOT (page 92)
MALBEC (page 98)
PRIMITIVO (page 113)

Grapes producing full-bodied, bold red wines with high, gripping tannins:
CABERNET SAUVIGNON (page 90)
SYRAH (page 94)
NEBBIOLO (page 102)

WHITE WINE

White wines vary from light and refreshing to concentrated and oaked. Some are best served as thirst-quenching aperitifs, with or without food. More complex and powerful styles of white are best served with rich dishes, and some can even make a good match for red meat. White wines range in colour from a pale, almost translucent green-yellow to a deep, golden honey colour.

White winemaking uses just the pulp of white grapes and not the skins. However, some winemakers may choose to leave the pulp in contact with the grape skins for a period in order to extract a bit of extra flavour and texture from them. A small number of white wines are made from red grapes by carefully crushing the grapes and quickly separating the juice from the skins – one example is the use of the red grape PINOT NOIR to produce (white) champagne.

KEY STYLES OF WHITE WINE

Grapes producing fresh, mineral white wines:
CHARDONNAY (page 72)
ALBARIÑO (page 80)
MELON DE BOURGOGNE (page 86)

Grapes producing expressive, fruity, floral white wines:
SAUVIGNON BLANC (page 70)
RIESLING (page 74)
GEWÜRZTRAMINER (page 111)

Grapes producing rich or oaky white wines:
CHARDONNAY, oaked (page 72)
CHENIN BLANC, oaked or from old vines (page 78)
VIOGNIER (page 82)

ROSÉ WINE

Most rosé wines are made from red grapes, with the blush colour resulting from juice contact with the red grape skins. The depth of colour will depend on the method used and on how long the process lasts. Some rosés are made by blending white and red wines, but this is not generally permitted in quality wines. A key exception is champagne, which (along with other traditional-method sparkling wines) allows for a proportion of red wine to be used in a blend to make the rosé style.

KEY ROSÉ WINEMAKING METHODS

Direct pressing

This method is often used for the palest styles of rosé. Once the red grapes are brought into the winery, they are gently pressed to separate the juice from the skins. This process extracts just a little bit of colour from the skins, along with delicate aromas and flavours.

Maceration

In this method, the red grapes are crushed and the juices are left to soak for a while with the skins (known as macerating) before being separated. Alongside colour, aromas and flavours, a little bit of tannin will also be extracted from the skins during the maceration period, which can vary in length from a few hours for pale rosés to a couple of days for deeper-hued styles.

STYLES OF ROSÉ

The popularity of very pale rosés has grown exponentially since around 2010. For many, this pale, peach-coloured wine is as much about the look as it is about the taste. The subtle pastel shades of this style are often associated with a chic and aspirational lifestyle – think oversized sunglasses and lounging on beach beds at exclusive St-Tropez clubs. Have you noticed how rosé bottles are usually made from clear glass to show off the wine's colour? Provence is the home of light-hued rosés, but they have been emulated all over Mediterranean Europe and further afield.

There is a common misconception that all deep-hued rosés are sweeter and lower in quality than pale rosés. This is certainly not the case. In some retailers, you might come across the confusingly named 'White Zinfandel' wines, which are in fact a type of rosé and usually entry-level in price and quality. These wines are deep-pink in hue

and off-dry to sweeter in style, but don't let them put you off other, deep-hued rosés. There are some premium styles of darker rosé with lots of flavour and character that have a distinctly dry finish, such as those from the southern Rhône region of TAVEL, and from various regions in Spain, which also deserve a place on the best beach club wine lists.

The classic southern French grapes used for rosé are GRENACHE, CINSAULT and MOURVÈDRE. However, rosés may be made from a variety of grapes depending on the region. For example, elsewhere in France PINOT NOIR and CABERNET FRANC are used, TEMPRANILLO is popular in Spain, and SANGIOVESE in Italy.

Rosés come in a variety of styles, but they are generally unoaked. Common aromas and flavours include delicate floral notes, red-berry fruit, such as strawberry and raspberry, stone fruit, such as white peach, as well as melon and watermelon. They may also have mineral notes of wet stones and a saline freshness.

Most rosés are intended to be drunk within a year or two of being made so that their fruity flavours and fresh character shine. I've been caught out before with a beautiful Provence rosé I ordered at a beach bar. I didn't notice that it was five years old – the colour was fine and it was a well-known producer, so I accepted the wine without trying it, poured out a couple of glasses and started sipping, only to be disappointed by

its muted flavours and stale finish. Lesson learned! So make sure you check the vintage when ordering rosé and be wary of those with bottle age. If you are in a shop or restaurant and the rosé is a bit older, check if there is a more recent vintage or if the ageing is intentional to complement a specific style.

ORANGE WINE

Orange wines, also known as amber wines, skin-contact wines or skin-fermented wines, have a fairly unusual profile, in that they marry the aromas and flavours of a rich white wine with the body of a red wine.

They may seem like a recent trend in the wine world, but orange wines are not a new phenomenon. Their history goes back some 8,000 years to Georgia, in the Caucasus, where wines of this type were made in large amphorae (known as *qvevri*) that were buried in the ground, with the skins acting as a natural preservative. Despite the name, these wines are in no way made from oranges, but you may pick up on some warm citrus notes – it's a common flavour descriptor. Other common aromas and flavours in orange wines include citrus peel, apricot and honey; nuances of perfume, tea and spices; nutty hints; and sometimes a savoury and salty character.

ORANGE WINEMAKING

Broadly speaking, orange wines are white wines made in the same way as red wines. Whereas in typical white wine production, white grapes are crushed and the juice is then quickly separated from the skins, in orange wine production, the white grape juice is left in contact with the skins for much longer. Colour and tannin are extracted from the skins, so these wines can vary from a light golden hue to a deep amber colour, depending on how long this process lasts – which can be anything from days (as with rosé wines) to several months. Tannin gives orange wines a more robust mouthfeel than white wines, so they pair well with flavour-packed recipes and meat dishes.

The modern orange wine movement centres around northern Italy and Slovenia, but there are many examples from across the world made from various white grapes, depending on their region.

SPARKLING WINE

Most wine drinkers can't help but feel joy on hearing that gentle pop of a cork, watching those brilliant bubbles fill a glass and taking a sip of that energetic effervescence.

Sparkling wines are often served in a celebratory context, but there are affordable styles that can be opened in more casual settings, and they are excellent with food too. The tiny bubbles are caused by dissolved carbon dioxide in the wine, and can vary from a gentle spritz to foamy and frothy or fine and persistent. There are several ways in which bubbles are made in sparkling wines, and here we will look at the two key methods: the traditional method and the tank method.

TRADITIONAL METHOD

The labour-intensive yet magical way in which the perfect tiny bubbles are formed in champagne was allegedly discovered by the Benedictine monk Dom Pérignon in the 17th century. Legend has it that he exclaimed, 'Come quickly, I am tasting the stars!' on first witnessing the remarkable sparkle. Today, this account is disputed, and some believe that the traditional method may not have been discovered in CHAMPAGNE at all but further south, in the region of LIMOUX. However, it's generally agreed that Dom Pérignon was a pioneer in elevating the quality of traditional-method sparkling wines – so much so that champagne giant Moët & Chandon named their flagship wine after him. Let's have a closer look at this complex, expensive yet enchanting method of creating sparkling wine.

+ **Base wine and second fermentation:** A mixture primarily made up of yeast and sugar is added to a bottle of still wine (known as the base wine) to initiate a second fermentation.

+ **The creation of bubbles:** The wine is then sealed with a crown cap (as found on a beer bottle), and once the alcoholic fermentation starts, the carbon dioxide created during that process is trapped in the bottle and dissolves into the wine, creating bubbles.

+ **Lees contact:** After the second fermentation is complete, the newly created sparkling wine stays in contact with the dead yeast cells (known as lees) for a period typically ranging from nine months to several years, which adds a richer, creamier texture along with biscuity and brioche notes. This lees character is a key feature of traditional-method sparkling wines.

+ **Riddling and disgorgement:** Once the wine has spent the desired time in contact with the lees, a special method is employed to remove the lees from the bottle. This begins with a process known as riddling, which involves slowly turning the bottles at an angle to collect the lees in the neck of each one. This is followed by disgorgement, the process by which the lees are removed, generally by freezing the neck of the bottle, removing the crown cap and allowing the natural pressure of the bubbles to cause the lees to be expelled from the bottle.

+ Dosage and bottling: Before it is sealed with a cork, the sparkling wine may also be topped up with additional wine and adjusted with sugar (a process known as dosage) to create the final wine and desired sweetness level.

Also known as: Méthode traditionnelle, champagne method, Méthode champenoise.

Champagne, France

Style: Fine and persistent bubbles, with characteristically high acidity. Aromas and flavours can vary from delicate and fresh with subtle lees nuances (citrus fruit, green fruit, floral, mineral, light pastry notes) to rich and flavourful with a more dominant lees character (ripe green fruit, stone fruit, bready, brioche and nutty notes). Champagnes also come in rosé styles, which can bring aromas and flavours of red-berry fruit. It is typically made in *brut* (dry) to *brut nature* (very dry, with no added sugar) styles, but sweeter styles do exist. Many vintage styles (see page 63) made in the traditional method are suitable for extended ageing.

Key grapes: CHARDONNAY, PINOT NOIR and PINOT MEUNIER. Many champagnes are made from a blend of all three of these grapes, CHARDONNAY bringing citrus notes, elegance and finesse, PINOT NOIR bringing structure, fruit and perfume, and PINOT MEUNIER bringing softness, approachability and fruity flavours. See page 63 for blanc de blancs and blanc de noirs styles.
Price: Premium to ultra-premium.

Alternatives to champagne

Only wines produced in the region of CHAMPAGNE and adhering to its rules are permitted to label their wines as champagne (see more on wine regions and appellations on pages 169 and 172). However, outside this famous sparkling hub there are many other excellent traditional-method sparkling wine regions across the world. For superb value, look in particular at French crémant, Spanish cava and South African cap classique (I picked this for my wedding reception).

Here are some alternative regions and countries producing traditional-method sparkling wines to try:

+ France – crémant
+ Spain – *CAVA* and *CORPINNAT*
+ England – English sparkling wine
+ Italy – *FRANCIACORTA* and *TRENTO*
+ Germany – some sekts
+ South Africa – cap classique
+ Tasmania, Australia
+ California, USA.

TANK METHOD

The tank method is a quicker, less labour-intensive and more cost-effective way of creating sparkling wines than the traditional method. This is why tank wines, such as prosecco, are often markedly cheaper than many traditional-method wines.

Let's have a closer look at this method of creating sparkling wine.

+ Base wine and second fermentation: Large stainless-steel pressure tanks (rather than individual bottles, as is the case in the traditional method) are filled with the still base wine, and a second fermentation is initiated by adding the yeast and sugar mixture to the tank.

+ The creation of bubbles: The tank is sealed and once alcoholic fermentation starts, the carbon dioxide created during the fermentation process is trapped in the tank and dissolves into the wine, creating bubbles.

+ Limited lees contact: After the second fermentation is complete, the newly created sparkling wine does not usually spend time in contact with the lees, creating a fresh and fruity style of sparkling wine.

+ Bottling: The sparkling wine may be adjusted with sugar (known as dosage) to create the final wine before it is bottled under pressure and sealed with a cork.

Also known as: Charmat method and Metodo Italiano.

Prosecco, Italy

Style: Larger and frothier bubbles than champagne, with usually a lower level of acidity. As the method avoids extended lees contact, the aroma and flavour profiles are pure, fresh and fruity, displaying notes such as green and citrus fruit. It is typically made in brut to extra dry styles (see opposite). The majority of tank-method wines are not suitable for ageing and should be drunk while young.

Key grape: GLERA

Price: Inexpensive to mid-range.

COMMON SPARKLING WINE LABELLING TERMS

Sweetness

You will find an indication of the sweetness level of sparkling wines made in the EU by the term used on the label. These terms are adopted for many sparkling wines made around the world too:

+ Brut nature – bone dry
+ Extra brut – very dry
+ Brut – dry
+ Extra dry – medium dry
+ Dry – medium sweet
+ Demi-sec – sweet
+ Doux – very sweet

The driest styles are labelled as brut nature. With no detectable sweetness and no sugar added at the final stage of the winemaking process (no dosage), they're sometimes referred to as zero dosage wines and tend to have a chalky, mineral-fresh finish. The sweetest styles of sparkling are labelled as doux, but these are very rare and you will more commonly find semi-sweet demi-sec styles. Sweetness can be hard to detect in sparkling wines as they tend to have high acidity, which balances the sweetness and has the effect of masking it. However, most people tend to be able to detect sweetness from around the extra dry level.

Vintage vs. non-vintage

A sparkling wine labelled with the vintage (meaning the year of harvest) usually contains grapes harvested only from that particular year (just like a typical still wine). Vintage sparkling wines are often made only in exceptional years, when the conditions have been excellent and the grapes are top quality, with the goal of creating a complex and age-worthy style of sparkling wine. A sparkling wine labelled as non-vintage is made from wines from multiple vintages (that is to say, grapes harvested across multiple years) that are carefully stored at the winery. The aim of a non-vintage blend is to create a consistent house-style year after year that is not affected by the conditions of a particular vintage.

Style

Blanc de blancs is a sparkling wine made from white grapes only, such as CHARDONNAY. These wines are commonly recognized for their high acidity, complexity and poise, citrus notes and mineral quality.

Blanc de noirs is a sparkling wine made from red grapes only, such as PINOT NOIR. These wines are commonly recognized for their slightly darker or richer tinge in the glass (which is very nuanced), having a bit more softness and approachability than blanc de blancs, together with fruitier and more perfumed notes.

SWEET WINES

Sweet wines are wonderfully indulgent and delicious. Too often they are saved for special occasions, but I encourage you to treat yourself more regularly to this delightful style of wine.

Sweet wines vary from delicate, floral and honeyed to richly flavoured, waxy and unctuous. They are usually served at the end of a meal, to accompany cheese and dessert, but I often pick a sweet wine to have instead of a pudding.

HOW SWEET WINES ARE MADE

Concentrating natural grape sugars

Many of the world's premium styles of sweet wine are made from grapes affected by a fungus known as noble rot (*Botrytis cinerea*). Don't be put off! This (good) fungus helps produce enchanting wines, including those from the famous regions of SAUTERNES and TOKAJ, as well as many sweet German RIESLINGS. The rot forms in moist and misty conditions, piercing tiny holes into individual grapes. If warm and sunny conditions follow, these holes allow water to evaporate, thereby concentrating the sugars, acidity and flavours. Noble rot-affected grapes produce wines with honeyed, waxy and citrus-peel aromas and flavours. Other sweet wines produced by concentrating sugars are:

+ Late-harvest wines, where grapes are picked later in the growing season, allowing for natural evaporation of water.
+ Wines made from drying the grapes once they are harvested (again encouraging evaporation).
+ Icewine made from frozen grapes left on the vine into the winter, and which (once picked) are pressed in a way that separates the concentrated juices from the frozen water (see also page 217).

Stopping fermentation

Sweet wines can be made by stopping the fermentation process before the sugars naturally present in the grapes have been converted by yeast into alcohol and carbon dioxide. This can be done through the process of fortification (see page 66). When fortification takes place during the fermentation process, the yeast will naturally die once the alcohol level exceeds around 15% ABV. The fermentation process will stop, and any unconverted sugars will remain in the wine. This is how port wines are made. Fermentation can also be stopped by removing the yeast, which is typically achieved by using a filtration system.

Note: Some sweet wines are made by adding unfermented grape juice to increase the sugar content. This is not permitted in most wine regions for quality sweet wines.

FORTIFIED WINES

Fortified wines are sometimes viewed as a bit fusty and outdated – but, believe me, this category is exciting, unique and a joy to match with certain foods. Fortified wines come in a variety of distinctive styles, from dry through to sweet, and many can be aged for decades and even centuries...

Fortification is the process of adding further alcohol to a wine to raise the overall level of alcohol. Most fortified wines sit within 15–22% ABV. Traditionally, fortification was used to preserve wines for transportation over long distances, and that's why we find some key fortified wine regions along historic shipping routes.

Let's look at two styles of fortified wine, one made in Spain and the other in Portugal.

SHERRY

There is so much more to sherry than the inexpensive sweet 'cream' sherries popularized in the 1970s. Sherries are made in a range of interesting and distinctive styles, with many complex dry options in addition to sweeter styles. I am a huge fan, and hope that you, after reading this book, will be persuaded to discover (or rediscover) this sometimes misunderstood and underappreciated category of fortified wines too.

✦ **Region:** Sherry wines come from Andalusia in southern Spain, and sherry production is centred around a triangle of three cities – *JEREZ, SANLÚCAR DE BARRAMEDA* and *EL PUERTO DE SANTA MARÍA* – together known as the sherry triangle.

✦ **Styles:** Some sherries are aged under a layer of naturally present yeast called *flor*, which contributes uniquely tangy, almost salty notes to the wine. These wines (fino and manzanilla) are usually dry and light-coloured like a white wine, with refreshing and delicate flavours (nuts, herbs, flowers), accompanied by that distinctive yeasty tang. Sipping a chilled fino with a plate of anchovies under the warm Andalusian sun has to be one of my favourite wine experiences. Other styles are aged in large barrels that allow for gentle oxidation of the wines over time, bringing dried fruit, nut and wood nuances to the wines; these can vary in colour from golden to dark coffee-brown. Known as oloroso and **PEDRO XIMÉNEZ** (PX) sherries, the former is generally dry and the latter sweet. Some styles are aged in a combination of the two methods and bring elements of each to the wine. These are amontillado and some palo cortado sherries, both of which are generally dry.

PORT

Port wines are far more approachable and versatile than you might think, so please put to one side the traditional image of old-fashioned, deeply coloured and bold fortified wines served by waiters wearing white gloves at lavish dinners. While they are always sweet, port wines are made in a range of styles for different occasions and they absolutely have a place outside a banquet setting.

+ Region: Port wines are made in the *DOURO* region of northern Portugal. The famous port vineyards are positioned on steep terraced slopes on either side of the Douro River, with port production based in Porto and Vila Nova de Gaia.

+ Styles: Ruby ports are deep red in colour and range from fruitier styles (ruby and reserve) to those that are more complex and age-worthy (late bottled vintage 'LBV' and vintage). Tawny ports undergo long oxidative ageing, which gives them a tawny (brown) colour and nutty and caramel notes, with many styles aged for decades before release – my favourite style of port. White and rosé ports, which can be served with mixers or used in cocktails, are growing in popularity too.

Other examples of fortified wines:
MADEIRA (Portugal), vin doux naturel (France), *RUTHERGLEN* muscat (Australia).

KEY GRAPE VARIETIES

Thousands of different types of grapes are grown around the globe, but the vast majority of wines are made from a small number of key varieties. Here are profiles of 20 of the world's most popular grapes, starting with white grapes and **SAUVIGNON BLANC** overleaf and moving on to red grapes with **PINOT NOIR** on page 88.

See pages 110–13 for brief introductions to 30 other grape varieties, from Assyrtiko to Zinfandel.

SAUVIGNON BLANC

Sauvignon blanc produces wines full of vibrancy and freshness, so no wonder it's one of the world's most popular grape varieties. Most bottles can be relied on to offer a distinctly dry and refreshing unoaked white wine that's a real crowd-pleaser. I've spent many an evening with a trusty bottle of SAUVIGNON BLANC paired with salty snacks and a good tête-à-tête. But it can also be oaked, blended with other grapes and even used to make sweet wines.

PROFILE

Dry white wines that are high in acidity and packed full of zesty notes of lemon, lime and gooseberry, often accompanied by distinctive green bell pepper, asparagus or grassy notes and a mineral freshness reminiscent of wet stones. In warmer wine regions, SAUVIGNON BLANC can have a riper fruit character, bursting with tropical fruit notes, such as passion fruit, melon and pineapple.

KEY REGIONS
France

France is considered the home of SAUVIGNON BLANC, as the grape is believed to have originated in the LOIRE. The regions of SANCERRE and POUILLY-FUMÉ in the LOIRE are the benchmarks for classic, mineral-driven, top-quality SAUVIGNON BLANC, but they can come with a premium price tag. Nearby TOURAINE offers similarly approachable but more affordable options. BORDEAUX produces dry SAUVIGNON BLANC in a wide range of styles, from easy-drinking and fruity to barrel-fermented, rich and age-worthy,

typically having notes of ripe citrus, stone fruit and honey. The grape is also used in sweet wines in BORDEAUX, including in the wine region of SAUTERNES.

New Zealand

Sauvignon blanc's meteoric rise in New Zealand is one of the greatest grape triumphs of all time. MARLBOROUGH in the South Island is known for its world-class examples that exploded onto the export market in the 1980s. New Zealand SAUVIGNON BLANC usually has a riper, more exuberant profile than its French friends, with tropical-fruit notes and a herbaceous punctuation, while retaining that characteristic crispness.

USA

California produces a range of SAUVIGNON BLANC, from everyday styles produced in the CENTRAL VALLEY to quality, characterful styles that include both aromatic and crisp examples from cooler spots (such as parts of SONOMA) to richer, riper and sometimes oaked styles found in NAPA VALLEY.

Other notable countries: Australia, Chile and South Africa.

PAIRINGS

Goats' cheese and asparagus, Asian-inspired salads, fresh and herby fish and poultry dishes.

IF YOU LIKE SAUVIGNON BLANC...
Try BACCHUS, GRÜNER VELTLINER, VERDEJO.

Flavour-wheel categories: Green fruit, citrus fruit, tropical fruit, botanical, mineral.

CHARDONNAY

The chameleonic CHARDONNAY grape, which is behind the lean, mineral wines of CHABLIS, produces rich and enveloping wines in the New World and is the key white grape in CHAMPAGNE. The wines it makes range from inexpensive and easy-drinking to some of the most complex and prized in the world.

PROFILE
Dry white wines with medium-to-full body and a spectrum of flavours: in cooler climates, think citrus and orchard fruit with a mineral freshness; in warmer climates, think richer stone fruit and even tropical fruit, such as pineapple and mango. Many chardonnays are oaked, which can give toasty and vanilla flavours. Winemakers may also allow malolactic conversion (see page 42) to take place, which gives a buttery and creamy character, and/or lees ageing (see page 43) for a richer texture and brioche-like notes. With age, CHARDONNAY can develop subtle flavours of honey, nuts and mushroom.

KEY REGIONS
France
BURGUNDY is the home of the ultimate expression of CHARDONNAY. CHABLIS in the north produces crisp and steely styles. Further south, the CÔTE DE BEAUNE is known for richer, elegant oaked styles from famous villages such as PULIGNY-MONTRACHET or MEURSAULT. Just south, the CÔTE CHALONNAISE is home to similar, slightly more wallet-friendly alternatives, and further south is the MÂCONNAIS, with riper, more attractively priced examples. The term 'white Burgundy' is generally used to refer to oaked styles from the area covering the CÔTE D'OR, CÔTE CHALONNAISE and MÂCONNAIS, whereas CHABLIS, given its stylistic difference, is typically referred to separately. Many of the best CHARDONNAYS across BURGUNDY come from vineyards classified as premier cru or grand cru.

USA
Many inexpensive styles come from California's warm CENTRAL VALLEY, while premium examples from SONOMA VALLEY and NAPA VALLEY vary from restrained in style to rich and full-bodied, with tropical fruit and a prominent oak character. Oregon is known for quality Burgundian-style CHARDONNAYS.

Australia
Australia produces a range of CHARDONNAY, from simple to top quality. YARRA VALLEY and MORNINGTON PENINSULA are known for elegant styles, as is MARGARET RIVER.

Chile
Great examples can be found in the regions of LIMARI, ACONCAGUA and CASABLANCA.

Other notable countries: England, Italy, New Zealand and South Africa.

PAIRINGS
Roast chicken, creamy pasta dishes, seafood and fish.

IF YOU LIKE CHARDONNAY...
Try ASSYRTIKO, CHENIN BLANC, GODELLO.

Flavour-wheel categories: Green fruit, citrus fruit, stone fruit, tropical fruit, mineral, dairy, wood.

RIESLING

RIESLING can have bright and unusual zippy fruit flavours and mouth-zinging acidity. This grape is often misunderstood, but in fact makes some of the best white wines in the world. It's loved by sommeliers and wine professionals alike for its aromatic intensity, variety of styles, range of sweetness levels and ability to age well. Let me reintroduce you...

PROFILE

An aromatic variety with an abundance of fruit and floral flavours; in cooler climates RIESLING displays zingy citrus, orchard fruit, white flowers and a steely quality. In warmer climates it can have peachy and riper floral notes, such as honeysuckle, blossom and even tropical fruit. It's generally unoaked so as not to disguise its aromatic qualities. Wherever it's grown, it has mouth-wateringly high acidity, giving freshness. RIESLING can vary from light in body and bone-dry in style to richly textured and lusciously sweet, with quality sweet versions made from late-harvested or noble rot-affected grapes. Some styles are suitable for ageing and can develop notes of honey, ginger and dried fruit – and also a kerosene note that 'petrol heads' (like me) love.

KEY REGIONS
Germany
The homeland of RIESLING, where it is made in a variety of styles at different sweetness levels. German labelling is complex, but you may see the following terms designating the sweetness of a wine: *trocken* (dry), *halbtrocken* (off-dry), *lieblich* (medium-sweet) and *süss* (sweet). The cool and steep region of MOSEL is known for world-celebrated delicate and mineral-driven RIESLING that can age for decades. RHEINGAU is slightly warmer, producing more body, and in the south, the warmer region of PFALZ makes richly textured and ripe styles.

France
Alsace has a reputation for quality RIESLINGS, ranging from dry to sweet, that share similarities with their German counterparts, and are known for their floral notes and mineral freshness.

Australia
EDEN VALLEY and CLARE VALLEY in South Australia produce premium ripe and zesty RIESLINGS that are usually dry or off-dry and can develop distinct petrol notes with age.

USA
The FINGER LAKES region in New York State is known for RIESLING at a range of sweetness levels and price points.

Other notable countries: Austria and New Zealand.

PAIRINGS
Medium-spiced Mexican recipes with dry styles, spicy Thai dishes with off-dry styles, cheese or fruit-based desserts with sweet styles.

IF YOU LIKE RIESLING...
Try ALBARIÑO, CHENIN BLANC, GEWÜRZTRAMINER.

Flavour-wheel categories: Green fruit, citrus fruit, stone fruit, tropical fruit, floral, sweet, mineral, smoke.

PINOT GRIGIO

The **PINOT GRIGIO** grape is known for producing crowd-pleasing, zesty wines that are great for sipping in a multitude of settings. No wonder it's so popular around the world! This is the first white I can remember buying from the local wine shop or at the pub during my university days. **PINOT GRIGIO** is synonymous with Italy but it's also an important variety in **ALSACE** in France, where it's known as **PINOT GRIS** and is famed for richer and more complex styles across a variety of sweetness levels. **PINOT GRIGIO** is classified as a white grape, but, unusually, it has a pink tinge to its skin.

PROFILE

Easy-drinking styles of Italian **PINOT GRIGIO** are dry, unoaked and light in body, with crisp apple and citrus flavours. Premium Italian examples have more body, complexity and riper fruit flavours, such as peach and apricot. Alsatian **PINOT GRIS** is often full-bodied in style with stone fruit and tropical flavours, such as mango, with spicy hints of ginger, honey and stones, and may be off-dry or sweeter. Quality styles of **PINOT GRIGIO** and **PINOT GRIS** may undergo lees ageing to add texture and weight to the wines. Some New World producers label their wines as **PINOT GRIS** to indicate that they are made in a richer style.

KEY REGIONS
Italy

Bottles of simple Italian **PINOT GRIGIO** can be found in shops and restaurants around the world, and these relatively neutral white wines are best served nice and chilled. They will often be labelled just as 'Italian pinot grigio' and made with grapes sourced widely from regions such as the **VENETO**. For examples of Italian **PINOT GRIGIO** with more oomph, texture and personality, look out for examples from specific regions, such as **ALTO ADIGE**, **COLLIO** and **FRIUILI COLLI ORIENTALI**.

France

ALSACE in eastern France has a reputation for high-quality, rich and age-worthy **PINOT GRIS** made in styles from dry to sweet. Some of the best wines in the region come from the 51 *grand cru* vineyards.

Other notable countries: Australia, New Zealand and the USA.

PAIRINGS

Easy-drinking styles are great with aperitif snacks or light salads, whereas rich and complex styles work well with white meat and fish dishes with an aromatic spicy or fruity element, such as chicken tagine.

IF YOU LIKE PINOT GRIGIO...
Try **ALBARIÑO, GAVI, PICPOUL.**

Flavour-wheel categories: Green fruit, citrus fruit, stone fruit, tropical fruit, mineral.

CHENIN BLANC

Versatile and underrated, CHENIN BLANC produces an array of wines from light and quaffable to rich and intense. I have a soft spot for this grape, which is made in a plethora of styles – dry, oaked, sweet and even sparkling. Easy-drinking styles make a charming aperitif, whereas complex dry styles pair superbly with a variety of foods, including fish, meat, spices and cheese. Sweet styles are delicious with pastry-based and fruity desserts.

PROFILE

Simple styles have flavours of apple and stone fruit, with a light body and medium-to-high acidity. Complex and richer styles are full-bodied and can show ripe peach and honeysuckle notes, while retaining high acidity and mineral freshness. Lees ageing contributes to doughy and pastry notes, while oak contact can give toasty notes. CHENIN BLANCS can have distinctive notes of hay and lanolin (like sheep's wool), which sounds a little odd, but balanced with expressive fruit and floral notes gives an appetizing earthy undertone. With age, it can become richer, honeyed and even take on a beeswax-like quality. CHENIN BLANC makes high-quality sweet wines from late harvest or noble rot-affected grapes, giving flavours of ripe apricot and citrus peel.

KEY REGIONS
France

The LOIRE is CHENIN BLANC's ancestral home. In TOURAINE, VOUVRAY is known for producing quality styles from still to sparkling and dry through to lusciously sweet. Further west, in ANJOU, SAVENNIÈRES is notable for premium dry and age-worthy wines, whereas COTEAUX DU LAYON nearby produces renowned sweet styles that rank among the best in the world. CHENIN BLANC is a key grape used in many crémants throughout the LOIRE region producing fruity, floral and approachable sparkling wines.

South Africa

The CHENIN BLANC grape has been hugely successful in South Africa, and accounts for some of the country's top white wines. SWARTLAND in particular is home to many a gifted winemaker fashioning complex, intense and age-worthy styles, often from dry-farmed old bush vines resulting in low yielding but highly concentrated fruit. South Africa also produces large quantities of everyday, simple and affordable CHENIN BLANC.

PAIRINGS

Salads and root vegetables (light dry styles), roast chicken, belly pork (rich dry styles), cheese board (rich dry to sweet styles), tarte tatin and similar desserts (sweet styles).

IF YOU LIKE CHENIN BLANC...
Try CHARDONNAY, RIESLING, VIOGNIER.

Flavour-wheel categories: Green fruit, citrus fruit, stone fruit, floral, sweet, mineral, wood, earth, bread.

ALBARIÑO

ALBARIÑO as it's known in Spain, or ALVARINHO over the border in Portugal, produces vivacious, fresh and crowd-pleasing wines that are hugely popular on the international scene. With its lively, fresh and saline character, it immediately transports me to a beachside shack with fish on the barbecue and the wind in my hair. Traditionally, ALBARIÑO has been celebrated for producing light and refreshing wines, but there are increasing numbers of winemakers exploring its ability to produce rich, complex and age-worthy styles.

PROFILE
Vibrant white wines with medium body and bright acidity bursting with citrus flavours of lemon and grapefruit, stone fruit, such as peach, white flowers and a saline, mineral quality. Riper styles have tropical-fruit notes, such as melon and pineapple. It can be made in a richer style using winemaking techniques, such as lees ageing, giving more body and texture. With its aromatic intensity and high acidity, some parallels have been drawn between ALBARIÑO and RIESLING.

KEY REGIONS
Spain
Originating from the coastal region of RÍAS BAIXAS in GALICIA, ALBARIÑO is the flagship grape here. It is known for citrusy, fresh and easy-drinking wines, but there are some producers making more richly textured, oaked styles with concentrated stone and tropical fruit. A small amount of sparkling wines are made from the grape too.

Portugal
One of the key grapes in the famous Portuguese region of VINHO VERDE, which translates as 'green wine', though the wines produced there are not green. This name is believed to refer either to the youthful paleness of the wines or the lush, verdant landscape from which they are sourced. ALVARINHO can be included in blends with other white grapes to make simple refreshing wines that have traditionally had a little spritz. Varietal ALVARINHOS can be labelled as VINHO VERDE ALVARINHO, showing off the characteristics of this grape.

PAIRINGS
Fresh shellfish, creamy seafood and fish, fried and salty tapas.

IF YOU LIKE ALBARIÑO...
Try GRÜNER VELTLINER, MELON DE BOURGOGNE, RIESLING.

Flavour-wheel categories: Citrus fruit, stone fruit, tropical fruit, mineral, floral.

VIOGNIER

If you like the idea of white wine that's voluptuous, exotic and decadent, it's time to get acquainted with VIOGNIER. Originating in the RHÔNE, this big, bold and beautiful grape flourishes under the sun in warm climates, but there are significant plantings in the New World too. It produces hypnotic wines that are high in alcohol, so make sure you take care when falling for this sultry white.

PROFILE

Rich and perfumed wines, with flavours of ripe stone fruit, citrus peel, floral notes and hints of spices, such as nutmeg and white pepper. Oaked styles can display vanilla and clove flavours. VIOGNIER is a great option for drinkers who prefer rich wines – and even those who normally drink only red wines. Like many reds, VIOGNIER can benefit from being served in a larger wine glass (sometimes even decanted) and just lightly chilled (rather than at colder fridge temperatures) to allow its aromatic qualities to open. It can accumulate high sugar levels in the vineyard, leading to potentially high alcohol (with some hitting 15% ABV), and coupled with its naturally low acidity, this can lead to wines that feel a bit flat and even oily on the palate. Premium styles carefully balance alcohol, acidity and this grape's intense flavours, and can age for decades, developing honey notes and a complex perfume.

KEY REGIONS
France

The NORTHERN RHÔNE produces some of the finest expressions, and CONDRIEU is dedicated to 100% VIOGNIER, producing intense whites from low-yielding old vines. Interestingly, some red-producing NORTHERN RHÔNE wine regions permit a small percentage of VIOGNIER to be blended with SYRAH to add perfume and to stabilize SYRAH's colour. Elsewhere in this region, VIOGNIER is blended with MARSANNE and ROUSSANNE to produce textured white wines. It is also present in the warm SOUTHERN RHÔNE and LANGUEDOC, and is typically used in white blends at various price points.

USA

There has been a notable increase in plantings of VIOGNIER in CALIFORNIA. Look out for quality examples from PASO ROBLES made in a varietal style, as well as in white blends.

Australia

Australia produces VIOGNIER at a range of price points and styles – from fresh, fruity and gently spiced to rich and gastronomic.

PAIRINGS

Roast chicken with all the trimmings, fruity and spiced dishes, such as a chicken and apricot tagine, medium-spiced fish or poultry curries.

IF YOU LIKE VIOGNIER...

Try MARSANNE/ROUSSANNE blends, oaked CHARDONNAY, rich CHENIN BLANC.

Flavour-wheel categories: Stone fruit, citrus fruit, floral, spice, wood.

GRÜNER VELTLINER

Fashionable GRÜNER VELTLINER – or grü-v (groovy!), as it's affectionally known in some quarters – is the flagship white grape of Austria. It's gained increasing admiration and popularity since the late 1990s, and today graces wine lists across the world with its approachable yet gastronomic and unique character. It has certain characteristics that resemble two of the world's most popular grapes: its textured body and citrus and stone fruit flavours are sometimes reminiscent of CHARDONNAY, while its high acidity and aromatic qualities bring to mind SAUVIGNON BLANC.

PROFILE

GRÜNER VELTLINER has crisp acidity and ranges in flavour from citrus fruit, such as lemon, lime and grapefruit, to riper styles with stone fruit flavours, such as peach and nectarine. It can have a subtle spicy and white pepper quality, along with vegetal and herb notes, such as celery and dill, giving it a unique profile. Easy-drinking, affordable styles are refreshing and fruity, whereas premium styles tend to be richer, fuller-bodied and can be aged to add complexity to the wines. It can be harvested late, giving intensity to the wines and allowing them to develop honey and ginger notes.

KEY REGIONS
Austria

GRÜNER VELTLINER is the key grape of Austria and is believed to be indigenous to the country. It thrives in NIEDERÖSTERREICH (Lower Austria), making a range of styles at different price points. Some of the best, premium expressions come from the region of WACHAU. Also look out for examples from KAMPTAL and WEINVIERTEL at a range of prices.

PAIRINGS

Vegetarian and herby salads, fried meat, such as the traditional schnitzel, creamy mushroom pasta or risotto.

IF YOU LIKE GRÜNER VELTLINER...
Try FURMINT, SAUVIGNON BLANC, VERDEJO.

Flavour-wheel categories: Citrus fruit, stone fruit, mineral, botanical, spice.

MELON DE BOURGOGNE

The lesser-known variety behind the much-loved and ever-popular white wine *MUSCADET* is MELON DE BOURGOGNE. This grape comes from the coastal region of the *LOIRE* and seems to bring a bit of sea essence to every glass. Take a sip and you'll smell that salty Atlantic air, hear the waves lapping and feel the sand between your toes. There is nothing quite like a bottle of chilled, refreshing *MUSCADET* served with fresh shellfish plucked straight from the ocean.

PROFILE
Alongside its hints of the sea are flavours of zesty lemon, apple, white flowers and a crushed shell-like quality, with high acidity and a saline finish. MELON DE BOURGOGNE wines are generally unoaked, light and versatile, making them great crowd-pleasers. Wines aged *sur lie* (on the lees) have a creamier and fuller texture, making them more gastronomic in style and great to pair with richer seafood dishes. Most *MUSCADET* wines are best served crisp and chilled, and are not intended to be aged.

KEY REGIONS
France
MUSCADET is situated in the far west of the *LOIRE*, in the wider region of *PAYS NANTAIS*. Confusingly, this region has a similar name to the aromatic variety MUSCAT (see page 110), but this grape isn't grown here and makes wines that are distinctly different to those made with MELON DE BOURGOGNE. While wines labelled as Muscadet are light and subtle, those labelled as MUSCADET SÈVRE ET MAINE come from an area with stricter regulations and tend to have a bit more character and concentration. Those labelled as 'sur lie' have more body and texture.

PAIRINGS
Fresh seafood platter, moules marinières, fish and chips.

IF YOU LIKE MELON DE BOURGOGNE...
Try ALBARIÑO, PICPOUL, PINOT GRIGIO.

Flavour-wheel categories: Citrus fruit, green fruit, mineral.

PINOT NOIR

Thanks to its thin skin, the PINOT NOIR grape is susceptible to disasters in the vineyard, which is why it's also known as 'the heartbreak grape'. With care and attention, it produces intensely fragrant and complex red wines that can be aged for a decade and beyond. It is often light-bodied with red-fruit flavours, and can have a perfumed and savoury quality that can make it challenging to enjoy at first if you are used to bold red wines. Take your time to appreciate its nuanced character, and you'll fall in love.

PROFILE

Classic PINOT NOIR wines are light in colour and body, with low silky tannins, fresh acidity and strawberry, cherry and raspberry flavours. With age, they can develop flavours of mushroom, autumnal undergrowth and game. Some winemakers use oak in the winemaking process, which can contribute toasty cedar and sweet cinnamon notes. This terroir-reflective grape can show interesting and nuanced differences depending on where it is grown.

KEY REGIONS
France

BURGUNDY is the key region for classic PINOT NOIR. The CÔTE DE NUITS in northern BURGUNDY contains world-renowned wine villages such as GEVREY-CHAMBERTIN, CHAMBOLLE-MUSIGNY and VOSNE-ROMANÉE. Many of the best wines come from specific vineyards classified as *premier cru* or *grand cru*. PINOT NOIR is also one of the main grape varieties used in champagne and traditional-method sparkling wines.

Germany

Germany produces quality PINOT NOIR known as SPÄTBURGUNDER. These wines tend to be light in colour and body, with high acidity and complex flavours. Look out for wines from BADEN, WÜRTTEMBERG and the AHR VALLEY.

New Zealand

New Zealand PINOT NOIR is typically medium-bodied and fruitier in style than examples from other countries, but still retains that fresh acidity. The wines are extremely accessible to a wide range of tastes because of their vibrant fruit character. Some great examples come from CENTRAL OTAGO, MARTINBOROUGH and MARLBOROUGH.

USA

CALIFORNIAN PINOT NOIR ranges from restrained and savoury to rich and fruity in style – check out top examples from SANTA BARBARA and SONOMA. OREGON has an ever-growing reputation for top wines made in a classic Burgundian style.

Australia

Cool parts of Australia, such as YARRA VALLEY and MORNINGTON PENINSULA, have a great reputation for sophisticated, fruit-driven PINOT NOIR.

PAIRINGS

Mushroom and truffle dishes, duck and game with fruity sauces.

IF YOU LIKE PINOT NOIR...

Try CINSAULT, GAMAY, NEBBIOLO.

Flavour-wheel categories: Red fruit, floral, earth, wood.

CABERNET SAUVIGNON

The world's most popular red grape, CABERNET SAUVIGNON originates from France, but is grown extensively across the globe today. It's the grape behind some of the most powerful, complex, age-worthy and expensive wines of BORDEAUX and NAPA VALLEY, and produces good-value reds in many New World countries, too.

PROFILE
This is a red grape that produces wines often described as structured, with its full body, high levels of tannin and rich flavours. This structure allows many styles to be aged for decades. It has black-fruit flavours, and can have nuances of mint or eucalyptus (from its parent, SAUVIGNON BLANC). It's often aged in oak, which contributes toasty, cedar and clove undertones. CABERNET SAUVIGNON can have a distinct graphite note, and with age develops tobacco, leather and coffee qualities. It can be made in a varietal style, but it's also blended with other red grapes in different regions.

KEY REGIONS
France
BORDEAUX is the home of CABERNET SAUVIGNON, where this grape is often blended with MERLOT and CABERNET FRANC (known as a BORDEAUX blend). It brings black fruit, tannin and acidity to a blend, and is the dominant grape of Left Bank wines – from the left (or southwest) side of the river Garonne. Here we find the MÉDOC region, which includes the famous appellations of ST-ESTÈPHE, PAUILLAC, ST-JULIEN and MARGAUX, known for complex and age-worthy styles.

USA
CALIFORNIA produces top CABERNET SAUVIGNON that can attract prices even higher than top BORDEAUX. STAGS LEAP DISTRICT, OAKVILLE and RUTHERFORD in NAPA VALLEY are particularly celebrated. With warmer temperatures, the styles made here typically have bolder fruit flavours, a fuller body and higher alcohol than those from France. WASHINGTON STATE also has a good reputation for quality CABERNET SAUVIGNON.

Australia
COONAWARRA and MARGARET RIVER produce CABERNET SAUVIGNON wines at a range of price points and styles with some premium expressions.

South Africa
STELLENBOSCH has a strong reputation for well-priced, quality CABERNET SAUVIGNON, often made in a BORDEAUX-blend style.

Chile
Great value and fruity, Chile's CABERNET SAUVIGNON can have a distinct blackcurrant note.

Other notable countries: Argentina, Italy and New Zealand.

PAIRINGS
Meat dishes in particular – steak, beef Wellington, boeuf bourguignon.

IF YOU LIKE CABERNET SAUVIGNON...
Try AGLIANICO, MALBEC, TEMPRANILLO.

Flavour-wheel categories: Black fruit, botanical, spice, wood, smoke, earth.

MERLOT

The international success of MERLOT has much to do with its fruity nature and smooth tannins, which give it a divine, mouth-hugging quality. Producing red wines that run the gamut from juicy, plump and affordable to complex fine wines that can attract eye-watering prices, MERLOT is made as a varietal wine but is also a key player in blends. Its popularity has ebbed and flowed over the years, with an expletive-laden rant about MERLOT in the 2004 film *Sideways* single-handedly causing a wobble in consumers' affections. But MERLOT is here to stay, with many great expressions found across the world.

PROFILE
Full-bodied wines with velvety tannins and a combination of fruit flavours ranging from red fruits, such as raspberry and cherry, to purple plums and blueberries, to black-fruit flavours. Oak use in winemaking can contribute vanilla, chocolatey and subtle, sweet spicy notes. Inexpensive MERLOT is a great fruity and food-friendly crowd-pleaser, while premium examples show more complexity of flavour and are capable of extended ageing.

KEY REGIONS
France
MERLOT originates from the BORDEAUX region, where it is grown throughout, but especially thrives on the Right Bank – on the right (or northeast) side of the river Dordogne. It is often blended with CABERNET SAUVIGNON and CABERNET FRANC, contributing red-fruit flavours, body and supple tannins. The Right Bank contains the world-famous wine regions of ST-ÉMILION and POMEROL. Premium and ultra-premium styles of MERLOT balance an elegant mouthfeel with intense flavour complexity. The wider BORDEAUX region also produces large volumes of inexpensive to mid-priced, fruity MERLOT-based wines.

USA
CALIFORNIA produces a range of MERLOT wines, from everyday, inexpensive ones to top-quality styles. The CENTRAL VALLEY generates many large-volume wines whereas NAPA VALLEY and SONOMA VALLEY are known for premium and complex styles.

Chile
Chile makes large volumes of good-value, easy-drinking styles, as well as more complex, ripe, mid-priced examples.

Other notable countries: Australia, Italy, New Zealand and South Africa.

PAIRINGS
Tomato-based meaty sauces, such as spaghetti bolognese, roast poultry and duck; grilled meats, such as barbecue ribs and burgers.

IF YOU LIKE MERLOT TRY...
Try GRENACHE, PRIMITIVO, SANGIOVESE.

Flavour-wheel categories: Red fruit, black fruit, wood, spice.

SYRAH

Seductive SYRAH is a multifaceted grape known for perfumed and peppery styles from France's NORTHERN RHÔNE, and ripe and unabashed styles from Australia, where it's commonly known as SHIRAZ. Depending on my mood and the occasion, I'll serve a voluptuous and bold SHIRAZ at a casual barbecue, and pair a subtle and savoury SYRAH with more elevated fare.

PROFILE

Like CABERNET SAUVIGNON, SYRAH has high tannins and acidity, and dominant black-fruit flavours, such as blackberry and blackcurrant. The traditional cooler-climate style is characterized by notes of violet perfume, peppery spice and smoky meat, as well as briny notes like those of olives and Mediterranean herbs. In warmer regions, SYRAH is bolder and riper, with a jammy fruit character and spicy and meaty notes too. It's also a key player in GSM blends: GRENACHE brings red fruit, spice and body, SYRAH brings black fruit and structure, and MOURVÈDRE brings meaty notes and power.

KEY REGIONS
France

SYRAH is the key red grape of the NORTHERN RHÔNE, and CÔTE-RÔTIE, HERMITAGE and CORNAS are three of the appellations there making top-quality SYRAH packed with elegant fruit and savoury flavours. Many of the wines from this region are complex, can be aged for decades and therefore attract a premium price tag, but there are also producers making more accessible examples, particularly in CROZES-HERMITAGE

and ST-JOSEPH. Many producers in the NORTHERN RHÔNE are careful about the use of new oak barrels so as not to disguise syrah's aromatics. Instead, they use large, older barrels that don't impart strong flavours to the wine. In the SOUTHERN RHÔNE and LANGUEDOC-ROUSSILLON, SYRAH plays a key part in GSM blends or variations.

Australia

BAROSSA VALLEY is known for producing ripe and full-bodied SHIRAZ with high alcohol and intense black fruit, plus meaty and chocolatey notes. Wines from this region often have toasty and sweet-spice notes from oak. Cooler parts of Australia, such as GEELONG in VICTORIA, produce styles like those in the NORTHERN RHÔNE.

USA

CALIFORNIA produces a range from savoury and peppery to fruity. An organization known as the Rhone Rangers champions RHÔNE styles, primarily in PASO ROBLES, but also further afield and into other US states.

Other notable countries: Chile, New Zealand and South Africa.

PAIRINGS

Rosemary-infused roast leg of lamb, spicy barbecue pork ribs, beef burgers with smoky bacon.

IF YOU LIKE SYRAH...
Try AGLIANICO, CABERNET SAUVIGNON, MALBEC.

Flavour-wheel categories: Black fruit, mineral, floral, spice, earth, stewed fruit.

GRENACHE

I think of GRENACHE as the warm and spicy relative of PINOT NOIR. Like PINOT, it can have low and silky tannins, a light colour and red-fruit-dominant flavours, but it loves the sun, producing high-alcohol wines that are often accompanied by intriguing spice notes. GRENACHE is used in some of the most renowned and powerful reds from France and Spain (where it's known as GARNACHA). It is integral to many fresh rosés from across the Mediterranean and capable of making light and ethereal reds, too.

PROFILE

Packed with berry-fruit flavours like ripe strawberry and raspberry, it can take on a baked or jammy fruit character in warm vintages and, with age, can develop rich, boozy fruit-cake notes. It can often have white pepper and spicy undertones, which add complexity and balance the fruity flavours. It is lower in tannins and acidity than other red grapes and can develop high levels of alcohol, so quality styles aim to balance alcohol and acidity with fruit flavours. In rosés, it's typically blended with other grapes and brings red-fruit flavours; it's also used in GSM blends (see page 94).

KEY REGIONS
France

A key variety in CÔTES DU RHÔNE red wines, which are often GSM blends. CÔTES DU RHÔNE covers a broad area across the RHÔNE VALLEY, producing a range of styles at different price points. It is also an important player in some famous regions of the SOUTHERN RHÔNE, most notably CHÂTEAUNEUF-DU-PAPE, where

it's central in blends but may also be made into a varietal wine. CHÂTEAUNEUF wines are typically powerful and age-worthy, with layers of baked fruit and complex spice, and attract premium prices. GRENACHE is one of the main red grapes used to make the pale rosés of PROVENCE, which are typically subtly fruity with a mineral freshness. The LANGUEDOC produces great-value GSM blends, and GRENACHE rosé.

Spain

Many PRIORAT red wines contain GARNACHA in the blend. It's hot in this region and vines are planted on steep, rocky slopes that are worked by hand. Here, gnarly old GARNACHA vines produce intense, berry-fruited and spicy wines, which have a premium reputation and are expensive. It is used in RIOJA alongside the key grape TEMPRANILLO. Varietal wine is made in the mountainous regions near MADRID, and these wines are often vibrant and light in colour, bursting with fresh berry fruit and delicate spice – very different from the robust wines of PRIORAT.

Other notable countries: Australia, South Africa and the USA.

PAIRINGS

Gamey dishes and duck with powerful styles; fish dishes, such as baked salmon, with lighter styles.

IF YOU LIKE GRENACHE...
Try CINSAULT, NEBBIOLO, PINOT NOIR.

Flavour-wheel categories: Red fruit, spice, stewed fruit, dried fruit.

MALBEC

Known for inky red wines with intense berry flavours that are adored across the world, MALBEC is recognizable, comforting and a real crowd-pleaser. It's synonymous with Argentina – there are few better pairings than a juicy MALBEC served with a perfectly charred yet tender steak – so it may come as a surprise that this grape originates from France. It was one the traditional grapes used in red BORDEAUX wines, but over time plantings have decreased due to its unpredictability in the region.

PROFILE

Full-bodied red wines with luscious dark-berry fruit flavours, such as blackberry and black cherry, often with a purple hue. MALBEC usually has medium levels of plush tannin and medium acidity, which make it smooth and velvety, and approachable for a wide range of palates. Some examples can show violet floral notes while ripe styles can have a rich chocolatey quality. When oaked, MALBEC can be accompanied by toasty and vanilla notes, and with age it can develop leather and coffee characteristics. From France, it typically has a more restrained and savoury flavour profile.

KEY REGIONS
Argentina

Introduced from France in the mid-19th century, MALBEC has been an incredible success in Argentina. It comes in a variety of styles, ranging from fresh and fruity wines for young consumption to rich and complex oaked styles that benefit from ageing. MALBEC is often made as a varietal wine, but may also be blended with other grapes, including CABERNET SAUVIGNON and SYRAH. Some of the best examples come from high-altitude sites in MENDOZA, which produce rich yet fresh styles – look out for quality examples from the subregions of UCO VALLEY and LUJÁN DE CUYO. Lower altitude sites in MENDOZA produce fruity, easy-drinking styles at affordable prices.

France

One of the classic red grapes used in red BORDEAUX blends, today MALBEC makes up only a tiny number of plantings in the region. In CAHORS in southwest France, it is the key red grape producing medium-to-full-bodied styles that have berry fruit flavours often accompanied by savoury earth, herb and meaty qualities.

PAIRINGS

Steak and barbecue meats, meaty pizza and pasta dishes. Vegetarian dishes such as miso aubergine or smoky barbecue veggies.

IF YOU LIKE MALBEC...
Try CABERNET SAUVIGNON, CARMENÈRE, SYRAH.

Flavour-wheel categories: Black fruit, floral, wood, earth.

TEMPRANILLO

The flagship red grape of Spain and a key variety in the much-loved red wines of *RIOJA*, TEMPRANILLO is highly successful on the international market due to its food-friendly nature, range of styles and excellent value, even at the premium end. I've had many a wonderful evening with friends, hearty food and a bottle (or several!) of TEMPRANILLO. Its name means 'little early one', a reference to its early ripening character compared to its vineyard companions. It's also grown in Portugal, where it's known as TINTA RORIZ, and is used in port wines, as well as still red wines.

PROFILE
Medium-to-full-bodied red wines with a combination of red- and black-fruit flavours, such as red cherry, plums, figs and blackberry. TEMPRANILLO can also display savoury notes of tomato and dried Mediterranean herbs, and can have noticeable tannins and acidity, depending on where it is grown and the style of winemaking. TEMPRANILLO is often aged in oak, which can contribute clove and vanilla notes; many styles are made for ageing, and over time develop flavours of leather and tobacco.

KEY REGIONS
Spain
RIOJA is one of the most recognized and loved wine regions across the world. TEMPRANILLO is its key grape and may be made as a varietal wine or blended with GARNACHA and smaller proportions of other red grapes. *RIOJA* wines are classified according to how long they've been aged in the barrel and the bottle. Joven wines are the youngest style, without ageing requirements, and are fruity and fresh. Then come Crianza, Reserva and Gran Reserva, which require increasing levels of ageing in barrel and bottle before release as you move through the classification. The use of American oak is traditional in the region and characteristically gives vanilla and coconut flavours compared to the spicy and cedar notes of French oak. *RIBERA DEL DUERO* is known for producing full-bodied and robust TEMPRANILLO wines, often labelled as Tinto Fino. TEMPRANILLO also produces berry-fruited rosés in Spain and good-value, juicy reds in central and southern Spain.

Portugal
TINTA RORIZ is one of the key red varieties used in the fortified wine, port. It is also used to make dry, full-bodied red wines in the *DOURO VALLEY* and *DÃO*.

PAIRINGS
Paella and tapas with fruity styles; tomato-based dishes with medium-body styles; grilled meats and rich dishes with complex and aged styles.

IF YOU LIKE TEMPRANILLO...
Try CABERNET SAUVIGNON, MALBEC, SANGIOVESE.

Flavour-wheel categories: Red fruit, black fruit, wood, smoke, earth.

NEBBIOLO

Powerful yet subtle, earthy yet floral, NEBBIOLO is native to Italy's *PIEDMONT* region and offers many sensory experiences in one glass. I love its captivating heady and alluring perfume, but beware...this mesmerizing charmer delivers serious power on the palate, with its mouth-puckering tannins and acidity. NEBBIOLO most often benefits from being aged, allowing its structure to integrate with its complex fragrance and flavours. It can develop leathery and mushroom notes, so is a classic pairing with the region's famous white truffle dishes.

PROFILE

Interestingly, despite its naturally high acidity and tannins, NEBBIOLO produces wines that are relatively light in colour and quickly fade to a brick-like orange after a few years of ageing. In its youth, it has flavours of red fruits, such as cherries and raspberries, and delicate notes of rose petals. With age, NEBBIOLO develops earthy notes of leather and (famously) tar – deliciously appetizing in the glass, even if it sounds unusual – and can take on a mushroom, almost truffle-like quality, making it a fantastic pairing with similarly flavoured dishes. Like PINOT NOIR, it is often considered to produce wines reflective of its terroir.

KEY REGIONS
Italy

BAROLO is the most famous region for premium, complex styles of NEBBIOLO, and these wines attract high prices given their quality and prestige. Wines bearing the *BAROLO* label are required to be aged for at least three years before being released to the market, with those labelled Riserva having been aged for at least five years. Many wines benefit from further extended ageing in the bottle to soften them. The nearby region of *BARBARESCO* also produces premium NEBBIOLO wines. Wines from *BARBARESCO* have shorter ageing requirements and are usually more approachable than *BAROLO*, though many still command high prices. Fruitier, more affordable and accessible styles of NEBBIOLO can be found in the wider region of the *LANGHE* in Piedmont.

PAIRINGS

Risotto or pasta with fresh truffle, game birds and meats, grilled steak and portobello mushroom.

IF YOU LIKE NEBBIOLO...

Try GRENACHE, PINOT NOIR, XINOMAVRO.

Flavour-wheel categories: Red fruit, floral, smoke, earth.

SANGIOVESE

This native Italian grape is the star behind some of the country's most adored wines. SANGIOVESE thrives under the Tuscan sun, resulting in scintillating red wines brimming with fruit and savoury notes. It produces a range of red wines, from simple table wines to rich and complex wines made for epicurean feasts.

PROFILE

SANGIOVESE has high acidity and gripping tannins, with flavours of red cherries, cranberry and plums. Fruit notes are typically accompanied with savoury flavours of tomato and herbs, such as thyme and oregano. With age, it can develop meaty, leathery, gamey and smoke flavours. It is often aged in oak, contributing sweet, spicy notes.

KEY REGIONS
Italy

TUSCANY is the key region for this celebrated grape, where CHIANTI – lying between Florence and Siena – is one of the most recognizable wine regions in the world making reds based on SANGIOVESE. These vary in quality and price: those labelled just Chianti tend to be affordable and simple, and can be quite rustic in style; those labelled Chianti Classico are adorned with an easily spotted black rooster on the label (a nod to a legendary historic dispute between Florence and Siena). Classico wines are considered higher quality and are subject to tighter regulations. You may also see Riserva on the label, which indicates further ageing requirements, and Gran Selezione, which designates wines at the top of the hierarchy – these are required to come from a single vineyard. Further south, SANGIOVESE is the main grape used in wines from VINO NOBILE DI MONTEPULCIANO, while BRUNELLO DI MONTALCINO wines are pure SANGIOVESE. Both regions are recognized for quality wines that undergo long ageing in barrel and bottle, with the best examples producing rich, complex and structured wines that can be aged for decades. 'Super Tuscan' wines may blend SANGIOVESE with international varieties; this movement gathered momentum in the 1970s, embracing non-indigenous Italian varieties, such as CABERNET SAUVIGNON and MERLOT, that weren't permitted in TUSCANY's key appellations, such as CHIANTI. These wines were labelled under the broad TOSCANA appellation, usually reserved for simple wines, but these wines were premium-quality and age-worthy, and quickly garnered international admiration. Today, some Super Tuscan wines are labelled under the new coastal appellation of BOLGHERI, which permits the use of international grapes, while many others are still labelled under TOSCANA.

PAIRINGS

Tomato-based Italian classics, charcuterie and hard Italian cheese, such as Pecorino Toscano, bistecca alla Fiorentina, grilled meats with Mediterranean herbs.

IF YOU LIKE SANGIOVESE...
Try CABERNET SAUVIGNON, SYRAH, TEMPRANILLO.

Flavour-wheel categories: Red fruit, botanical, wood, earth.

CABERNET FRANC

The parent of two of the world's most recognized red grapes — MERLOT and CABERNET SAUVIGNON — 'CAB FRANC' is an underrated red grape often overshadowed by its children. It produces youthful, floral and fragrant wines, as well as layered and age-worthy wines. Lighter styles can be served slightly chilled and make a great aperitif or sipping red, whereas more complex styles are superb food wines.

PROFILE

This grape produces medium-bodied red wines, with medium grippy tannins and bright acidity. It's packed with red-fruit flavours, such as raspberry and cherry, and black-fruit flavours, such as blackcurrant, and it can have floral notes of violet. It can show quite 'green' qualities which vary from underripe stalky nuances to more attractive leafy, bell pepper and dried herbs. These are often accompanied by a gravelly, mineral quality. Many of the best examples balance fruity and floral notes with approachable savoury characteristics. It is also a player in BORDEAUX-style blends, bringing a softer texture and floral note.

KEY REGIONS
France

The CABERNET FRANC grape is believed to originate from BORDEAUX, where it generally plays a supporting role in MERLOT and CABERNET SAUVIGNON blends. However, there are some revered wines that use a higher proportion of the grape. In the LOIRE, it's the key red grape, making a range of wines from the fresh and drinkable through to the complex. Some of the best examples come from SAUMUR-CHAMPIGNY (in SAUMUR), BOURGUEIL and CHINON (in TOURAINE). It is also used in crémant and in fruity rosé wines across the LOIRE.

Other notable countries: Canada, Italy and the USA.

PAIRINGS

Confit duck leg with cranberry sauce, smoked meats, nut roasts and mushroom dishes.

IF YOU LIKE CABERNET FRANC...

Try CABERNET SAUVIGNON, RHÔNE SYRAH, MENCÍA.

Flavour-wheel categories: Red fruit, black fruit, floral, mineral, botanical.

GAMAY

This is the grape behind France's *BEAUJOLAIS* wine region, famous for its cheeky, playful and fruity reds, but the real gems are its more muscular and concentrated styles, which can rival expensive *BURGUNDIAN* *PINOT* *NOIR*. Many expressions are delightful served lightly chilled to keep their juicy red-berry flavours fresh and vibrant, making them appetizing summer reds. Lighter styles are great as an aperitif, and can work well with fish, whereas more complex styles can be paired with richer dishes.

PROFILE

GAMAY produces wines with a light-to-medium body, soft tannins and fresh acidity. Lighter styles are bursting with red-fruit flavours, such as strawberry and raspberry, and some winemakers use a technique (called carbonic maceration, and variants of it) that brings out lively bubblegum and banana flavours. More complex styles may display black-fruit flavours of blueberry and blackcurrant, which can be accompanied by floral violet notes, savoury smoke, iron and earthy qualities.

KEY REGIONS
France
The history of *GAMAY* in *BEAUJOLAIS* dates back almost 1,000 years, but its popularity has fluctuated over that time. The 20th century brought international love for 'Nouveau' styles, but for a period the region was known only for these simple and fruity wines. Today there is greater appreciation for a more nuanced range of styles, and *GAMAY* has become increasingly fashionable in the context of consumer preference trending towards lower alcohol and lighter reds. In terms of labelling, Beaujolais Nouveau wines are young and fruity in style, while Beaujolais wines are approachable with a little more fruit concentration than Nouveau wines. Next in the hierarchy are Beaujolais Villages wines, which come from an area comprising 38 villages and typically display more structure and depth of flavour. Beaujolais Cru wines are made from grapes from one of ten specific *crus* (villages) and have the highest reputation for quality. These are complex and age-worthy styles, with some examples capable of ageing for ten years or more. Some well-known *crus* are *ST-AMOUR*, *FLEURIE*, *MORGON* and *BROUILLY*. Outside *BEAUJOLAIS*, there are some small plantings in the *LOIRE* and *BURGUNDY* too.

PAIRINGS
Cheese and charcuterie, herby roast salmon or sea bass, duck and poultry dishes with aromatic spices or red fruit sauces.

IF YOU LIKE GAMAY...
Try *BLAUFRÄNKISCH*, *FRAPPATO*, *PINOT NOIR*.

Flavour-wheel categories: Red fruit, floral, mineral.

OTHER WHITE GRAPES

Here is a selection of other white grapes, listed from broadly lightest to boldest in style.

✦ **Bacchus:** Germanic grape now with major plantings in England, producing dry, fresh wines with elderflower, lemon and garden-herb notes.

✦ **Cortese:** The grape behind Italy's popular *GAVI* wines, producing dry and citrusy styles with high acidity.

✦ **Garganega:** Produces Italy's *SOAVE* wines, delightfully dry with orchard and stone fruit notes. Some of the best examples are labelled as *SOAVE CLASSICO*.

✦ **Verdicchio:** Italian grape producing fresh and fruity dry, light white wines with apple and lemon flavours.

✦ **Verdejo:** Spanish grape primarily grown in the *RUEDA* region, making dry, fresh and aromatic whites similar to *SAUVIGNON BLANC*, with some more textured and oaked styles too.

✦ **Picpoul:** Grown primarily in France's *LANGUEDOC* region, with plantings elsewhere in France and Spain, produces zesty, dry white wines.

✦ **Assyrtiko:** A high-quality Greek grape with naturally high acidity, producing dry wines with a mineral-fresh quality, citrus and stone-fruit flavours, and also the specialist sweet wine Vinsanto from *SANTORINI*.

✦ **Furmint:** The flagship grape of Hungary is used in the famous sweet wines of *TOKAJ*, and also increasingly to produce dry wines with flavours of orchard fruit and spice, and high acidity.

✦ **Muscat:** The name given to a family of grapes grown in many regions, characterized by their intense perfumed flavours of rose and blossom. Made in dry, sweet and sparkling styles.

✦ **Palomino:** The key grape used in fortified sherry wines (see page 66), with some producers now also using it to make small quantities of dry white wine.

✦ **Godello:** A high-quality Spanish white grape that is often compared to CHARDONNAY, making a range of fresh through to richer styles of wine, with ageing potential.

✦ **Sémillon:** Made in a range of dry through to sweet white wines, including as a key player in the famed sweet wines (as well as dry styles) of BORDEAUX. It's also known for quality wines in Australia's HUNTER VALLEY region.

✦ **Roussanne:** Found primarily in France's RHÔNE VALLEY, producing dry, fragrant and perfumed whites, and is typically blended with MARSANNE. It is also found in the USA (predominantly CALIFORNIA).

✦ **Marsanne:** Produces dry wines with weight and rich fruit flavours; it's typically blended with ROUSSANNE in France's RHÔNE VALLEY. Like ROUSSANNE, it's found in the USA too (predominantly CALIFORNIA).

✦ **Gewürztraminer:** Known for full-bodied, rich and intensely perfumed whites that can be high in alcohol, with flavours of lychee, rose and baking spices. Made in dry through to sweet styles.

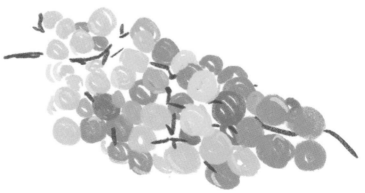

OTHER RED GRAPES

Here is a selection of other red grapes, listed from broadly lightest to boldest in style.

+ Frappato: Native to SICILY, this grape is used in blends and made as a varietal wine that has a light body, fresh and fragrant red-fruit flavours and vibrant colour.

+ Cinsault: Traditionally used as a supporting grape in red and rosé blends in southern France, but can also make interesting light varietal wines with flavours of red berries and spice. There are sizeable plantings in South Africa too.

+ Barbera: From PIEDMONT in northern Italy, with bright acidity, moderate tannins and red-cherry and strawberry flavours plus hints of spice.

+ Corvina: The grape behind Italy's fruity and fresh wines from VALPOLICELLA, and used in rich Amarone wines (made in a range from dry to sweet), where it gains intensity of flavour through the process of drying the grapes once picked.

+ Blaufränkisch: Quality grape grown mainly in Austria, producing medium-bodied wines with fresh acidity and flavours of black berry fruits and spice.

+ Mencía: Found in northwest Spain (and Portugal, where it is known as JAEN), making quality wines in both fruity and simple styles, as well as complex and age-worthy ones, with red fruits, floral and herbaceous notes.

+ Nero d'Avola: The key red grape of SICILY, made in styles ranging from easy-drinking to concentrated and age-worthy, with rich berry and plum fruit, herbs and spice.

+ Xinomavro: A high-quality grape from Greece that is often compared to NEBBIOLO, having high tannins, acidity and flavours of red berries, herbs and earthiness.

+ Pinotage: Created in the early 20th century in South Africa from a genetic crossing between PINOT NOIR and CINSAULT grapes, producing full-bodied, richly fruited and spiced reds ranging in quality.

+ Carmenère: The flagship grape of Chile, where it produces full-bodied red wines with dark-berry fruit flavours; it originated in BORDEAUX, where it historically played a minor role in blends.

+ Montepulciano: The grape in the popular MONTEPULCIANO D'ABRUZZO wines from central Italy, known for producing rich, bold red wines with juicy and ripe berry flavours, and also some lighter, fruity styles.

+ **Zinfandel/Primitivo:** Found in the USA as ZINFANDEL and Italy's *PUGLIA* as PRIMITIVO, producing full-bodied, high-alcohol wines with smooth tannins, rich and ripe berry fruit flavours and sweet spices.

+ **Mourvèdre:** A key grape in southern France, also grown in Spain, where it's known as MONASTRELL. Often blended with GRENACHE and SYRAH, to which it brings colour, rich fruit and meaty notes.

+ **Aglianico:** A quality grape from southern Italy, producing full-bodied, high-tannin and age-worthy wines with dark-berry notes, and developing earthy, meaty and spicy notes with age.

+ **Touriga Nacional:** Flagship Portuguese grape used in port wines and quality, age-worthy dry red wines, principally in the *DOURO* region; with deep colour, high tannins and bold flavours of black fruit.

THE MAGIC
OF FOOD AND
WINE

GENERAL PRINCIPLES OF FOOD AND WINE PAIRING

My philosophy for food and wine pairing is to experiment, lean into your instincts and have fun in the process. Food pairings are my favourite part of the world of wine – and I believe the key to this experience is sensory enjoyment and not worrying too much about strict rules. As a helpful starting point, let's look below at some

Food element	Example	Considerations
Flavour	Light and delicate Deep and intense	Match foods with wines of equal intensity of flavour so that one does not overpower the other. You're seeking a balance of flavour intensity, not a battle.
Texture	Silky Crunchy Viscous	For an interesting gastronomic experience, think about contrasting and complementary textures. Viscous textured food can work well with light wines, for example. Wines high in tannins can overpower delicate textures, so consider pairing them with steak or lamb, the density and fat content of which will soften tannins.
Sweet	Chocolate Fruit Desserts	The principle for pairing wine with sweet dishes is to match the food with wines that are just as sweet, because dry wines can feel bitter and acidic.
Salt	Savoury snacks Soy-based dishes Cheese	Salt brings out the fruit flavours in wine and increases the perception of a wine's body, so a dry white wine will taste fruitier and have more texture when paired with salty food. If you like the combination of salt and sweet, try pairing a sweet wine with cheese.

broad principles for matching food with wine. Then we'll delve into different food categories, with a selection of my favourite simple recipe and wine pairings to enjoy at home, and finish by looking at wines to pair with flavours from around the world.

Pairing examples

MUSCADET and shellfish both have fresh and delicate flavours.
SANGIOVESE and lasagne both have robust and intense flavours.

Contrasting textures, such as crunchy fried snacks and a light PINOT GRIGIO. Complementary textures, such as succulent chicken breast and a buttery CHARDONNAY, or a high tannin CABERNET SAUVIGNON and a steak.

A rich, sweet port and chocolate.
Sparkling sweet and fruity MOSCATO D'ASTI with fruit-based desserts.
Sweet and honeyed CHENIN BLANC and almond cake.

Refreshing SAUVIGNON BLANC with salty nuts and crisps.
Dry and bright CHABLIS and sushi.
Unctuously sweet SAUTERNES and cheese.

Food element	Example	Considerations
Acid	Vinaigrette Lemon Tomatoes	Acidity in food complements wine by bringing out all the fruity flavours. I like to pair high-acid dishes with high-acid wines, as I enjoy the complementary refreshing quality and how it makes the fruit flavours pop.
Fat	Deep-fried food Creamy dishes Cheesy recipes	Wines with high acidity pair well with fatty dishes, as the acidity cuts through the fat, providing a satisfying contrast and a refreshing finish.
Spice	Mustard Chilli Aromatic spices	Foods with a spicy kick increase our perception of alcohol, which can make a wine feel unbalanced or lead to a burning sensation, so consider lower alcohol, fruity wines. If you like the combination of sweet and spicy, try an off-dry or sweet wine. Very spicy and rich curries will overpower wines, so consider a refreshing beer or fruity cocktail instead.
Umami	Mushroom and truffle Eggs Cheese Shellfish Meat Soy and miso	Umami-rich foods have a meaty and savoury quality. In cooking, this character is often balanced by salt or acidity (see above), which makes them easier to pair with wines. Umami-rich dishes can make wines feel bitter and dry, so I like to pair them with fruity wines. I may also consider pairing these dishes with wines that have similar savoury flavours.

Pairing examples

A bright and fresh ALBARIÑO or SAUVIGNON BLANC served with grilled fish and fresh lemon. High-acidity red FRAPPATO and pasta with tomato sauce.

With fatty food, consider *CHAMPAGNE* and similar high-acidity sparkling wines and high-acidity white wines, such as SAUVIGNON BLANC, some CHARDONNAY and ALBARIÑO.

Off-dry RIESLING or CHENIN BLANC and a medium-spiced green curry.
Spicy meat ribs with a fruity red, such as a *BEAUJOLAIS*.

Miso aubergine and a fruity PINOT NOIR.
Mushroom risotto with an earthy *BAROLO*.
Omelette with a fruity sparkling wine, such as a French crémant.

APERITIFS AND CANAPÉS

An apéritif is a drink served before dinner that is typically light and refreshing in nature, with the purpose of awakening our senses and stimulating our appetite. Enjoying an aperitif at the end of the day is one of life's simple but joyful pleasures.

So which wines fit the bill? As an aperitif is likely to be the first drink sipped that day, possibly on an empty stomach, you'll want to avoid a wine that is too powerful or intensely flavoured. Generally, it's appealing to serve wines in a crescendo of intensity and boldness. So for that first drink, many of us enjoy something white that is light and refreshing, such as an unoaked white, like those from Italy, a *CHABLIS*-style **CHARDONNAY**, or a mineral-driven **SAUVIGNON BLANC**, such as *SANCERRE*. Alternatively, try a fresh fino or manzanilla sherry, and of course you can never go wrong with a glass of chilled sparkling wine. Dry rosé wines are a great option if you prefer something a little fruitier with a bit more body.

Crisps, olives and nuts

With simple salty or briny snacks, my go-to pairings are the refreshing white wine, sherry and sparkling aperitif suggestions above. Salt brings out the fruitiness of a wine and increases our sense of its body, so these wines will taste expressive, textured and refreshing when served alongside casual nibbles at the end of a long day.

Crudités and dip

Choosing white wines that have herby or garden-vegetable nuances creates a harmony between the wine and the ingredients on your crudité platter. If you've put together a board with veggies, such as bell peppers, celery, radishes and blanched asparagus, try pairing it with white grapes such as **SAUVIGNON BLANC**, **GRÜNER VELTLINER** and **BACCHUS**.

Charcuterie and cheese

I like to pair charcuterie and cheese with refreshing wines that have a bit more oomph and body to stand up to the intensity of flavours, fat content and saltiness. My favourite wallet-friendly option is a rich style of vintage cava – honestly the best way to start an evening – either white or rosé style. Other rich styles of traditional-method sparkling wines work well too. Lightly chilled, low-tannin reds (such as PINOT NOIR) and richer and oaked whites (such as CHENIN BLANC) are also great options. Consider dry sherries too – lighter fino and manzanilla work with fresh flavours, whereas richer amontillado, palo cortado and oloroso can stand up to deep and intense flavours.

Deep-fried snacks

I find that deep-fried snacks, such as arancini and croquetas, are best served with fresh wines with high acidity to cut through the fat and lift that crispy consistency – I like that contrast. Excellent options include fresh Spanish wines, such as an ALBARIÑO or a TXAKOLI (see page 217 for more on this grape). If you like the idea of playing with texture, I'd recommend pairing sparkling wines with fried snacks for an exciting, palate-stimulating contrast between the bubbles and the crunch of the food.

Tapas board paired with sherry

I love putting together a tapas-style board to serve when I'm having friends over for casual drinks. I like to pick a combination of fresh and rich ingredients, and I usually have quite a few salty snacks on the board too.

A thirst-quenching dry sherry served fridge-cold is a delightful match. A dry fino or manzanilla is a great-value and widely available option, and I adore their refreshingly tangy, almost salty character with these snacks. Alternatively, if you prefer to stick to white wine or sparkling, consider pairing your tapas board with a fresh, unoaked white or dry cava.

How to build your tapas board

I like to create a board that looks fabulous and tastes great too. Think colour, texture and a range of flavours. Start with a small bowl in the middle of the board and build the ingredients around this central point like a fan. Then place some of the ingredients in a range of different little dishes to add interest, and I will fill any gaps on the board with some fresh rosemary from the garden. There are no other rules – just have fun and get creative.

Quick and easy tapas board ideas

+ Salted Marcona almonds (or a cheeky hack is to rub regular blanched almonds in a few drops of olive oil with a pinch of fine sea salt).
+ Tomato bread made from toast topped with blitzed tomato, garlic, olive oil and salt.
+ Large olives, each wrapped in a fresh anchovy and held together with a cocktail stick.
+ Cold prawns marinated in garlic, lemon, chopped parsley and cracked black pepper.
+ Slices of Manchego cheese cut in triangular slices with the rind at the shortest edge.
+ Blanched asparagus with paprika aïoli.

POULTRY

CHICKEN

When it comes to wine pairings, chicken is incredibly versatile. It has a naturally mellow flavour, but also some density and texture, which means it can be paired with whites, rosés and light-to-medium reds, and even orange and sparkling wines. The key considerations are how it is cooked and which other ingredients are used. Chicken can be poached, roasted, or deep-fried; cooked simply with salt and herbs, or dressed up with creamy sauces or aromatic spices. The cooking method and ingredients will guide your wine choice.

Roast chicken

The perfect roast chicken has flavour, fat and texture, with the gorgeous crunch of salty, crispy skin to balance the succulent meat. My go-to wines are full-bodied whites and light-to-medium-bodied reds that stand up to the richness of the chicken but won't overpower it. For whites, try classic oaked CHARDONNAY from France or the New World, rich South African CHENIN BLANC or VIOGNIER, or Spain's white RIOJA or GODELLO. For reds, lighter styles, such as PINOT NOIR or BEAUJOLAIS work well, as do bright Italian reds, such as Sicilian FRAPPATO. You can also try light styles of CINSAULT (there are great ones from South Africa) and fresh styles of GRENACHE (look for high-altitude examples from central Spain).

Fried chicken

Hear me out on this one! The ultimate wine pairing with a bucket of greasy fried chicken is a chilled bottle of champagne. Fast food and fine fizz give the ultimate sensory buzz. There's something incredibly satisfying about the way the freshness of champagne, with its prickle of bubbles, cuts right through the crumb and fat of fried chicken. For wallet-friendly alternatives, try Spanish cava or French crémant. Alternatively, white or Provence-style pale rosé wines with high acidity work well, too.

Light chicken dishes

Pair chicken salads with unoaked whites or rosés for a light and refreshing experience and avoid overpowering these dishes with a bold wine. I also recommend fresh Italian whites with bright citrus flavours and mineral finishes, such as PINOT GRIGIO (head to ALTO ADIGE for wines with personality) or try SOAVE, VERDICCHIO or GAVI. A classic unoaked CHARDONNAY (such as CHABLIS), or a similarly bright ALBARIÑO from Spain, are reliable choices. Pale rosés are great too, with their delicate fruit and floral flavours.

Creamy chicken

Pair creamy dishes with similarly textured whites that have good acidity to balance the cream. Go for oaked CHARDONNAY from BURGUNDY or cooler New World spots, such as VICTORIA in Australia, ELGIN or WALKER BAY in South Africa and OREGON in the USA.

DUCK

Duck leg, pan-seared breast and crispy aromatic duck with pancakes are some of my all-time favourite dishes. PINOT NOIR is my choice wine with duck, as I adore how its fruity and savoury character balances the rich flavour of the meat, and how its high acidity cuts through the fattiness. Both Burgundian, restrained styles of PINOT NOIR and fruit-forward New World styles work well. Peppery *NORTHERN RHÔNE* SYRAH and more robust styles of *BEAUJOLAIS* are another great option – look out for *BEAUJOLAIS* Cru wines from *MORGON* and *MOULIN-À-VENT*, and you can find similar characteristics in an Austrian BLAUFRÄNKISCH. Consider pairing dishes, such as duck à l'orange, with aromatic whites with depth, which can echo flavours of the dish, such as rich styles of PINOT GRIS and GEWÜRZTRAMINER.

TURKEY

The brown meat in turkey has a richer flavour and denser texture than chicken. A whole roast turkey is often served in a celebratory context, so it's good to pick wines that can stand up to the flavours and richness of all the accompaniments. Classic pairings include mature (bottle-aged) *BORDEAUX*-style red wines that combine fruit and savoury flavours, red GSM blends that combine fruit, herbs and spice, and full-bodied, oaked CHARDONNAY and other similarly rich styles of white. If you'd like to keep to red but are keen to pair with something less oaky and fresher in style, try a Spanish MENCÍA or *LOIRE* CABERNET FRANC, which are typically medium-bodied and combine attractive berry fruit flavours with wild-herb notes.

GAME BIRDS

Game birds, such as pheasant, partridge and grouse, have a smoky and slightly wild flavour. I like to pair them with a range of fragrant red wines that have equally complex flavours and pick up on their earthy qualities. Mature PINOT NOIR, combining fruit and a savoury character, is a favourite, but also consider NEBBIOLO with its intriguing flavours of plum, rose, tar and (with age) truffle. A restrained and peppery *RHÔNE* style of SYRAH is another delicious match, as is a GSM blend.

Five-spice duck leg and plum salad paired with pinot noir

Duck and **PINOT NOIR** are a timeless pairing. I love the use of five-spice in this recipe as it brings out some of those delightful sweet and woody aromas, and spices (such as clove, cinnamon and star anise) that are common in oaked styles of **PINOT NOIR**. There's also a really satisfying symmetry in the sweetness from the cooked plums and the savoury, smoky character from the duck with the fruity, spicy and earthy flavours you can find in **PINOT NOIR**.

Serves 2

2 duck legs, skin-on
2 tablespoons five-spice
    powder
1 teaspoon olive oil
salt and pepper

For the salad

3 ripe plums, pitted and
    quartered
80g (3oz) watercress
1/2 small cucumber, cut into
    long thin strips
2 spring onions (scallions),
    cut finely lengthways
2 tablespoons toasted
    cashew nuts, roughly
    chopped
handful of fresh coriander
    leaves (cilantro)

For the dressing

3 tablespoons soy sauce
1 tablespoon olive oil
1 tablespoon sesame oil
1/4 lime
1 tablespoon honey

Preheat the oven to 180°C (160°C fan), 350°F, Gas Mark 4. Remove the duck legs from the fridge and pat dry with kitchen paper, then score all over with a sharp knife. Season each duck leg with a tablespoon of five-spice powder and some salt and pepper. Place in a roasting tray in the oven for 80 minutes, until crisp on the outside.

Meanwhile, heat the olive oil in a small frying pan (skillet) over a low heat. Add the plums, cut-side down, and cook gently until lightly caramelized. Remove from the heat and set aside.

Prepare the salad on two plates. Begin with the watercress, followed by the cucumber strips and the plums. Top with the spring onions, cashew nuts and coriander leaves.

Combine the ingredients for the dressing in a small pan and bring to a rapid boil, then remove from the heat and allow to cool.

Once the duck is cooked, remove from the oven and leave to rest for 10-15 minutes. Plate the duck next to the salad. Drizzle the dressing all over and serve.

MEAT

Let's look at four categories of meat – beef, lamb, game and pork – and consider some mouth-watering pairings.

BEEF

Beef is full of flavour and umami, with a robust texture and, depending on the cut, a high fat content too. Generally, beef is best paired with red wines, and it has a particularly positive interaction with high-tannin styles. Tannins bind to the dense protein content of beef, which softens their feel, while protein also brings out the fruit flavours in a wine, giving an overall sensation of balance. Reds that have acidity present work well in lifting the heaviness of fat in many beef dishes.

CABERNET SAUVIGNON from BORDEAUX and New World countries, such as the USA, South Africa and Australia, with their dark-berry flavours, high tannins and acidity, are classic pairings with beef dishes, from roasts to beef Wellington, grilled steak to hamburgers. Also consider other similar styles of red wine, such as RIOJA Reserva and Gran Reserva, quality CHIANTI and Super Tuscan wines, crowd-pleasing MONTEPULCIANO D'ABRUZZO, southern Italian AGLIANICO, peppery styles of SYRAH, as well as juicy New World SHIRAZ, Argentinian MALBEC and powerful Portuguese reds from regions such as the DOURO.

Slow-cooked, braised and stewed beef recipes, such as short ribs, ragu or bolognese, are great with the reds above, but also consider pairing with more plush, juicy and velvety reds, such as MERLOT, and Italian favourites, such as a rich Italian Amarone or a brooding Puglian PRIMITIVO.

Raw dishes, such as beef tartare and carpaccio, or just-seared beef dishes are exceptions to the above suggestions, as they typically have a more delicate flavour profile and texture. I would avoid pairing these dishes with bold reds and would instead look to lighter or earthier reds, such as PINOT NOIR or NEBBIOLO. But if you're feeling experimental, I have also tried these types of dishes with complex, aged CHARDONNAYS and rich white and rosé champagne, which all make exquisite matches.

LAMB

Lamb naturally has a gamier, slightly sweeter flavour than beef, and most cuts usually have a higher fat content. Similar red wines to my beef suggestions above will work well, but I particularly like to pair lamb with reds with a bit of spice or a mineral quality to mirror my favourite lamb seasonings, such as pepper, smoky herbs and garlic, and briny ingredients, such as olives, capers and anchovies. Some of my top picks with lamb include Rhône-style SYRAH, GSM blends, BEAUJOLAIS Cru, savoury styles of PINOT NOIR (like those from the village of GEVREY-CHAMBERTIN in BURGUNDY, which sometimes have an iron-like quality) and earthy Greek XINOMAVRO. For slow-cooked lamb dishes with a fruity element, such as a tagine, I'll also consider pairing with a full-bodied, flavourful and spiced white, such as a rich style of VIOGNIER.

GAME

Like game birds, game meats – such as venison and wild boar – have a stronger, earthier and more savoury flavour than other meats, so pair with reds that have similar qualities, such as mature PINOT NOIR or NEBBIOLO, which start to develop those intriguing mushroom and forest-floor notes. A mature SANGIOVESE is also a delicious option. For something different, try with a nutty and toasty oloroso sherry. You can always rely on my suggestions for beef too.

PORK

Pork is generally considered a white meat. Its flavour is milder than the red meats in this section, with the best dishes showing off its juicy, succulent and tender character. Depending on the cut, pork can have some marbling and fat. As with my suggestions for roast chicken (see page 124), my top picks with pork are full-bodied whites, light-to-medium-bodied reds and versatile rosés. With a gently spiced pork belly or herby porchetta, consider wines with similar notes to complement the dishes. My top picks are a light GRENACHE, which can have white-pepper notes, and reds that can display delicious herby undertones, such as medium-bodied styles of SANGIOVESE, a *LOIRE* CABERNET FRANC or Spanish MENCÍA. Asian-inspired pork dishes that use ingredients such as soy, ginger and honey are delicious with rich, dry styles of CHENIN BLANC and SÉMILLON – and you could even pick a fragrant orange wine too.

For more powerfully flavoured pork dishes, such as barbecue ribs or slow-cooked pulled pork, consider medium-to-full-bodied smooth reds with juicy fruit, such as spicy GSM blends, or the suggestions for slow-cooked, braised and stewed beef recipes opposite.

My top barbecue crowd-pleasers

Serving a mixture of meats, salads and accompaniments:
+ MALBEC
+ SYRAH/SHIRAZ
+ *BEAUJOLAIS*

White wines to pair with meat

Bold styles of whites to pair with meat for non-red drinkers:
+ Oaked styles of white *RIOJA*, CHARDONNAY and CHENIN BLANC
+ Rich styles of PINOT GRIS
+ VIOGNIER and *RHÔNE*-style white blends.

Slow-roast lamb paired with syrah

Serves 4
bone-in lamb shoulder
    (approx. 2kg/4lb)
olive oil or butter
1/2 bottle of inexpensive
    white wine
400g (14oz) can plum
    tomatoes
5 tablespoons pitted black
    olives
20g (3/4oz) fresh rosemary
    stalks
10g (1/3oz) fresh thyme
6 garlic cloves, sliced
100g (31/2oz) canned
    anchovy fillets, partially
    drained
salt and pepper
handful of chopped parsley,
    to serve

For the yogurt dip
170g (6oz) Greek yogurt
juice of 1/4 lemon
1/4 small cucumber, finely
    diced
2 tablespoons finely
    chopped mint
1 tablespoon honey

Side dishes
potato wedges, roasted
chickpeas and butter beans,
mashed potato, flatbreads,
mangetout and green
beans, sprouting broccoli,
charred lettuce

This juicy and tender, Mediterranean-inspired slow-roast lamb is an absolute dream served with a peppery *NORTHERN RHÔNE* SYRAH. You can also try similar styles of SYRAH from the New World, and GSM blends would work well too. I love the harmony of flavours you find in this style of SYRAH and this dish: black olives, saltiness, smoky herbs and earthy meat flavours.

Take the lamb out of the fridge 30 minutes before cooking. Rub the lamb with olive oil or butter, salt and pepper. Warm 2 tablespoons of olive oil in a large frying pan set over a medium heat, add the lamb to the pan and brown on all sides for around 5–6 minutes. Remove from the heat and set aside.

Preheat the oven to 150°C (130°C fan), 300°F, Gas Mark 2. Pour the white wine into a large ovenproof dish, then add the plum tomatoes, black olives, rosemary and thyme. Place the browned lamb on top.

Prick about 20 holes in the lamb and stuff each one with a sliver of garlic and half an anchovy fillet. Rub the lamb skin with 1 tablespoon of salt, 1/2 tablespoon of black pepper and some butter or olive oil.

Loosely wrap foil over the top of the dish and place the lamb in the oven for 4–5 hours, until the meat can be pulled apart easily with two forks.

Make a simple dip by combining the Greek yogurt, lemon juice, cucumber, mint and honey. Season to taste with black pepper. Serve the lamb with the dip and a selection of my suggested side dishes.

FISH AND SHELLFISH

This category covers many variations of flavours, textures and cooking techniques, so here we will look at some of the most readily available types of fish and seafood.

RAW AND CURED FISH AND SHELLFISH

I like to pair oysters and other raw and carpaccio-style fish and shellfish dishes with dry, mineral-driven whites with high acidity. Classic French examples are CHABLIS, SANCERRE, MUSCADET, PICPOUL, or from Italy SOAVE or VERDICCHIO, which all match the light and nuanced flavours and textures in the ingredients. Refreshing styles of sparkling wine – in particular drier Brut Nature and Extra Brut styles – are great options too, as are bright and tangy fino and manzanilla sherries. Cured fish, such as smoked salmon, has a richer flavour than fresh, so it can stand up to more flavourful styles of wines – still and sparkling rosés and more intensely aromatic whites, such as RIESLING and New Zealand SAUVIGNON BLANC.

SWEET AND DELICATE SHELLFISH

I love a chilled *plateau de fruits de mer* (seafood platter) with a gorgeous bottle of wine. Tucking into prawns, crevettes, langoustines, crab and lobster served simply with lemon and mayonnaise – is there anything more delicious? In their natural state, these types of shellfish have sweet and relatively delicate flavours, but get a little zing from a squeeze of citrus. When it comes to wine pairings, my suggestions for raw shellfish will work well, but also consider sparkling and white wines with a little more depth of flavour. These include subtly oaked styles of CHARDONNAY (from BURGUNDY, or similar styles from cool-climate New World wine regions), a Spanish ALBARIÑO or old-vine VERDEJO, and sparkling wines with more complexity, such as vintage blanc de blancs CHAMPAGNE, known for their poise and freshness.

DELICATE AND FLAKY FISH

White fish, such as cod, sole, plaice and sea bass, have a lovely flaky, melt-in-the-mouth texture when pan-fried, grilled or baked. These fish are usually best paired with medium-bodied white wines with a bit of texture and citrus and stone fruit flavours. Subtly oaked CHARDONNAY from BURGUNDY, SONOMA (California) or MARGARET RIVER (Australia) are always a sound choice, but if you are looking to branch out, try a Greek ASSYRTIKO or Spanish GODELLO, as these quality wines often share flavour and textural similarities with a trusty white CHARDONNAY.

FIRM AND FLAKY FISH

Fish such as salmon, turbot and halibut can stand up to ripe and oaked whites. Aside from oaked CHARDONNAY, consider CHENIN BLANC or VIOGNIER. Another firm favourite of mine is a rich style of SAUVIGNON BLANC from BORDEAUX – these wines are often blended with SÉMILLON and oaked, displaying stone fruit, honey florals, spice and a creamy texture (quite unrecognizable from a SANCERRE style of SAUVIGNON BLANC). Light-bodied and chilled reds, such as PINOT NOIR, BEAUJOLAIS, an Italian FRAPPATO, or fresh CINSAULT, will work a treat too, as will the opulent choice of a rosé champagne (particularly with salmon).

FIRM AND MEATY FISH AND SHELLFISH

Octopus, tuna and monkfish can stand up to bold and textured wines due to their meatier texture. Full-bodied CHARDONNAY will pair a treat, as will similarly powerful whites. Also consider deeply coloured, flavourful dry rosés and light-to-medium reds. You could even opt for a bolder red – not just a PINOT NOIR. I love pairing braised octopus with a medium-bodied Crianza style of *RIOJA*, or a Parma ham-wrapped monkfish with a fruity style of GRENACHE.

BRINY AND OILY FISH

I am 100 per cent addicted to anchovies and that's a good thing, because they are fantastic with wine. That salty character works a treat for enhancing a wine's fruit and freshness. Classic pairings with anchovies include refreshing dry, unoaked whites with a mineral quality (see my suggestions for raw fish on page 132) and refreshing fino and manzanilla Sherries. But you can also consider reds that have a briny, smoky, charred-herb character, especially where anchovies are used as an ingredient in a larger dish. One of my favourite pairings is a simple anchovy pizza with a *NORTHERN RHÔNE* style of SYRAH, or chilled, iron-like *BEAUJOLAIS*, or a herby, mineral Spanish MENCÍA. These wines will work with mackerel and sardines too.

FRIED FISH AND SHELLFISH

As with my suggestions for fried chicken on page 124, fried fish and shellfish dishes, such as battered cod, calamari and deep-fried soft-shell crab, pair superbly with a chilled bottle of bubbles. The high acidity found in traditional-method sparkling wines brings a delicious freshness and balance to fried dishes. Other refreshing whites, such as a MUSCADET, and light rosés with bright acidity will work a charm too.

OTHER FISH AND SHELLFISH CONSIDERATIONS

Your accompaniments and sauces may also influence your wine choice. Generally, citrus, butter and fresh herbs go well with white wine. See page 140 for pairing suggestions with tomato-based sauces and mushrooms, and pages 158–65 for international-cuisine considerations.

Pairing red wine with fish and shellfish

I am often asked if you can ever serve red wine with fish and shellfish – traditionally seen as the cardinal sin of pairing. My simple answer is YES. But you need to be mindful of tannins and flavours. Red wine's tannins can overpower subtle textures in fish and shellfish dishes, and when tannins interact with fish and shellfish oils, they can make them feel bitter. Bold red wine flavours can also dominate nuanced notes in these dishes. But some reds are an excellent option with fish and shellfish. I generally find the most successful have low and silky tannins, fresh fruity flavours and can be served lightly chilled.

Crab pasta paired with rosé

Serves 2

1 tablespoon olive oil
1 small onion, diced
2 garlic cloves, finely
    chopped
1 red chilli, finely chopped
1 fennel bulb, finely diced,
    keep the fennel fronds
    for serving
1 small glass white or rosé
    wine
400g (14oz) can cherry
    tomatoes
handful of parsley,
    finely chopped, plus
    extra to serve
juice of 1/2 lemon
150g (5oz) dried spaghetti
    or linguine
200g (7oz) white crab meat
100g (3 1/2oz) brown crab
    meat
3-4 tablespoons single or
    double cream (light or
    heavy cream) or crème
    fraîche (sour cream)
    (optional)
salt

To serve

2 tablespoons panko
    breadcrumbs, lightly
    fried
1 teaspoon lemon zest
fennel fronds, chopped
lemon wedges

This dish is made from just a few ingredients, but it tastes divine. I use brown and white crab meat for a combination of fresh, salty, sweet and slightly smoky flavours. My wine pick here is a rosé – either a pale Provence-style or a rosé with a bit of colour, like those from TAVEL in France. I love the berry-fruit nuances you find in a rosé with the juicy and slightly sweet flavours in the tomatoes and crab meat. Rosé wines also have a lovely crisp freshness that lifts the richness of the dish.

Warm the olive oil in a large frying pan set over a low heat, then sauté the onion until translucent. Add the garlic, chilli and diced fennel to the pan and season with salt. Cook for a couple of minutes, stirring continuously.

Add the wine, cherry tomatoes, chopped parsley and lemon juice to the pan. Simmer on a low heat to cook off the alcohol without reducing the sauce too much.

Meanwhile, cook your pasta until al dente in salted boiling water.

Add the drained pasta to the frying pan and stir in a little of the pasta water to loosen the sauce. Then take the pan off the heat and carefully stir in the white and brown crab meat. Add the cream or crème fraiche, if using.

Plate up and finish by sprinkling over the panko breadcrumbs, lemon zest, fennel fronds and some more chopped parsley. Serve with lemon wedges.

Salmon poké bowl paired with albariño

Serves 2
100g (3½oz) sushi rice
1 tablespoon rice wine
    vinegar (optional)
200g (7oz) sushi-grade
    salmon, diced
1 avocado, fan-sliced
5 tablespoons edamame
    beans
4 radishes, finely sliced
½ small carrot, peeled into
    ribbons
¼ small cucumber, finely
    chopped
100g (3½oz) mango,
    chopped

Dressing
4 tablespoons soy sauce
2 tablespoons mayonnaise
1 tablespoon sesame oil
1 tablespoon sriracha
juice of ½ lime

To serve
black sesame seeds
1 red chilli, finely chopped
1 tablespoon dried fried
    onions
coriander (cilantro) leaves
pickled ginger

Who doesn't love a poké bowl? I'm a big fan of their array of bright colours, healthy ingredients and lively textures. I like to pair them with a crisp style of white wine, so an **ALBARIÑO** is a great choice. It's packed with citrusy flavours and has a mineral, sea-like quality, which is delicious with the raw salmon and crunchy veg in this dish.

Begin by cooking the rice – you can use sticky white or brown rice instead of sushi rice, if you prefer. Once it has cooled, season with the rice wine vinegar, if you like, and divide between two bowls, ready to add your toppings.

Picture each bowl as a clock and, starting at 12pm, work your way around them, carefully placing portions of the ingredients next to each other on top of the rice. For this poké bowl, I've chosen salmon, avocado, edamame beans, radish, carrot ribbons, cucumber and mango – but you can easily substitute any of these items for other veg and tropical fruit. I like to vary the colours and textures for a rainbow-like effect.

Combine the ingredients for the dressing in a small bowl and stir until smooth. Drizzle a generous amount of the dressing over each poké bowl, and finish by decorating with black sesame seeds, chilli, dried fried onion, coriander and slices of pickled ginger.

VEGETARIAN AND VEGAN

Let's consider the best wines to go with popular vegetarian and vegan ingredients, thinking in particular about flavour intensity, texture, umami and acidity in this category.

EGGS

Eggs are naturally high in umami and have a rich yet subtle flavour, so I find they pair best with wines that have fresh acidity and moderately fruity notes that won't overpower them. Match brunch classics, such as omelettes, eggs Florentine and quiche, with easy-drinking, refreshing whites such as a mineral *MUSCADET*, zesty SAUVIGNON BLANC or unoaked CHARDONNAY. Another tried-and-tested-favourite is a bottle of perfectly chilled champagne.

TOMATOES

Many tomato-based dishes are wine-friendly, as they combine flavour and fresh acidity. With raw and fresh tomato dishes, consider pairing with crisp, high-acid whites and rosés to complement the similar qualities in the tomatoes. With richer and deeper tomato dishes, and those that combine stronger flavours, such as olives and herbs, go for crowd-pleasing, smooth reds, such as a youthful *RIOJA*, MERLOT or GSM blend. Italian reds (such as SANGIOVESE) are a great option too – as they say, what grows together goes together.

MUSHROOMS AND TRUFFLES

Mushroom and truffle flavours are a delight to pair with wine. Mushrooms have a mellow, earthy character, and truffles are

similar, but more intense. These umami-rich ingredients work well with red wines that have similar savoury characteristics alongside fruit flavours and fresh acidity (remember that umami can make a wine seem bitter, so wines with a fruity character generally work better). My suggested reds are NEBBIOLO or PINOT NOIR, or a mature *CHIANTI*. Another, more experimental, option is a dry amontillado or palo cortado sherry, which can show complex nutty, smoky and caramel notes. For a white wine option, try rich, oaked and aged styles of white, such as a white *RIOJA* or CHARDONNAY.

GOURDS AND ROOT VEGETABLES

Gourds and root vegetables, such as pumpkin, butternut squash, celeriac, carrots and turnip, typically balance nuanced savoury and sweet notes and, when cooked, can have a tender and velvety texture. I like to pair these ingredients with wines that match their flavour profile and texture. Light reds, such as PINOT NOIR, fit the bill, as do fragrant orange wines and honeyed and rich styles of white, such as VIOGNIER, CHENIN BLANC or PINOT GRIS.

ASPARAGUS, PEAS AND LEAFY GREENS

Asparagus is notoriously difficult to pair with wine as it has a combination of bitter, earthy and grassy flavours. But something magical happens when paired with SAUVIGNON BLANC. The two work harmoniously together. Alternatively, try other fresh-and-herby whites, such as Austrian GRÜNER

VELTLINER or Spanish **VERDEJO**. These whites go well with pea and leafy green dishes too, or consider other fresh, unoaked styles of white, such as **PICPOUL**, **VERDICCHIO** or **BACCHUS**, and unoaked **CHARDONNAY** is always a dependable choice.

AUBERGINE (EGGPLANT), GRAINS AND LEGUMES

These ingredients naturally have a savoury and rustic character. In cooking, they are extremely versatile and their texture and flavour will vary greatly, depending on the recipe. Texture can range from creamy to firm to crispy, depending on how they are cooked. Flavour-wise, they are often dressed up with other ingredients and spices, and can strongly take on the other flavours they are cooked with. The key considerations for pairing wines here is to think about the other elements in the dish and the cooking method.

TOFU

Tofu has a relatively neutral flavour, comes in a variety of textures from soft to firm, and can be cooked in many ways, including pan-fried, scrambled, baked, grilled or steamed. When pairing with wine, consider the other ingredients in the dish, any seasonings or marinades to be used, the texture of the tofu and the cooking method. Lighter and more delicate dishes will be best paired with wines sharing similar characteristics, and the same applies for heavier and richer tofu dishes.

SALADS

Salads come in a variety of styles, so a good starting point is to think the lighter the flavours, fat content and texture, the more delicate the wine pairing should be to match them. So, for example, fresh and crunchy salads with a citrusy vinaigrette pair well with wines sharing similar characteristics, such as youthful styles of sparkling wine and unoaked, light whites and rosés. For richer salads or those served with heavier or fattier dressings, consider bolder sparkling, white, rosé and orange wines. Generally, I avoid red wines with salads, unless the salad is vegetable-, grain- or legume-based.

What are vegan wines?

Eggs in my wine – you've got to be yolking! The fining process, through which naturally occurring (but unwanted) lumps and particles are removed from the wine, has traditionally included the use of non-vegan products, such as egg whites, milk and even dried fish bladders, because of their binding properties. However, today there are plenty of vegan substitutes, such as seaweed or volcanic clay, that can be used instead.

Asparagus and goats' cheese tart
paired with sauvignon blanc

Asparagus and **SAUVIGNON BLANC** is a match made in heaven. Loire expressions have a mineral freshness, citrus flavours and nuances of grass and garden herbs that make them a delightful pairing with this tricky vegetable. My tart recipe also includes goats' cheese, which is another classic combination with **SAUVIGNON BLANC**.

Serves 2–4

1 sheet ready-rolled puff pastry
5 tablespoons cream cheese
5 tablespoons salted butter, softened
zest of $1/4$ lemon
100g (3/2oz) goats' cheese, crumbled
350g (12oz) thin asparagus spears, trimmed
juice of $1/2$ lemon
olive oil
1 egg, beaten
1 tablespoon chopped flat-leaf parsley, to serve
salt and pepper

Preheat the oven to 200°C (180°C fan), 400°F, Gas Mark 6. Take the puff pastry from the fridge around 20 minutes before using. Place the sheet of pastry on a baking tray and use a blunt knife to lightly score a border about 1cm ($1/2$in) from the edge. Make a few gentle pricks with a fork in the middle of the pastry.

In a small bowl, mix together the cream cheese, butter and lemon zest. Using a blunt knife, carefully spread the cream cheese mixture over the puff pastry, keeping within the border.

Sprinkle half of the goats' cheese over the cream cheese mixture, then lay the asparagus spears over it – I like to do so in neat rows, or you can take a more free-form approach. Drizzle the lemon juice over the asparagus and then sprinkle with the remaining goats' cheese.

Season the tart with salt and pepper and drizzle with a little olive oil. Brush the border of the pastry with the beaten egg.

Bake for 20–25 minutes, until the puff pastry is golden and the goats' cheese is bubbling.

Sprinkle the chopped parsley over the tart and serve with a green salad.

Aubergine (eggplant) curry
paired with off-dry riesling

When it comes to curry, RIESLING is my go-to grape. This simple vegan curry with a moderate level of spice is an absolute delight to serve alongside this wine. RIESLING – especially one with a little bit of sweetness – works exceptionally well with dishes exhibiting some spice, as its expressive fruity, floral and sweet qualities provide an appetizing balance to fragrant dishes with heat. These wines usually have lower levels of alcohol too, so you'll avoid getting a burning sensation when pairing with hot spice.

Serves 4

1 onion, diced
2 tablespoons olive oil
3 garlic cloves, finely chopped
5cm (2in) piece of fresh root
    ginger, finely chopped
1 red chilli, finely chopped
2 tablespoons curry powder
1 tablespoon garam masala
8–10 curry leaves
2 large aubergines (egg-
    plants), cut into chunks
200g (7oz) canned chopped
    tomatoes
400ml (14fl oz) coconut milk
juice of 1/2 lemon
400g (14oz) can chickpeas,
    drained
100g (3 1/2oz) mangetout
    (snowpeas)
salt and pepper
fresh coriander leaves
    (cilantro), to serve

Accompaniments
steamed rice and/or
flatbreads, mango chutney,
coconut yogurt dip

In a deep frying pan (skillet) set over a low heat, sauté the onion in a tablespoon of the olive oil until translucent. Add the garlic, ginger, red chilli, curry powder, garam masala and curry leaves to the pan, then season with salt and pepper. Cook for a couple of minutes, stirring continuously, allowing the flavours to combine.

Add another tablespoon of olive oil and the aubergine to the pan. Increase the heat to medium and cook for a further few minutes. Keep stirring so that everything browns nicely but doesn't burn.

Once the aubergine has started to soften, add the tomatoes, coconut milk and lemon juice to the pan. Reduce the heat to medium-low and, once everthing is gently bubbling, add the chickpeas and allow to simmer for 5–7 minutes.

Add the mangetout to the pan and continue cooking for a few minutes, until all the vegetables have softened but still have a nice crunch.

Serve in bowls with a sprinkle of fresh coriander leaves to add colour, alongside some or all of the suggested accompaniments.

CHEESE

Cheese and wine – a union like no other. The flavours of cheese can range from subtle and creamy to strong and tangy, with many different variations on grassy, earthy, nutty notes and more – so consideration should be given to matching the intensity of cheese and wine. What else do we need to consider when pairing the two? First, cheese can have a high fat content, so wines with fresh acidity will give some lift to that fattiness. Cheese can also be high in salt, so it complements dry wines by bringing out their fruity flavours. For those who love a salt vs. sweet combination, the saltiness of cheese can also be enjoyable to pair with sweet wines. Texturally, cheese can vary from light and silky to coarse and grainy, so consider wines with complementary or contrasting textures for a sensory kick.

FRESH CHEESES

Mozzarella, burrata and ricotta are examples of young cheeses that have a fresh and creamy flavour and texture. My choice wines for these are fresh, mineral-driven pale rosé and white wines, such as an Italian *SOAVE* or a fresh GRÜNER VELTLINER, for an attractive symmetry in flavours and texture. With richer burrata dishes, amped up with ingredients, such as roasted veg or cured meat, consider light styles of orange wine too, which will bring fragrance and umami richness.

BLOOMY RIND CHEESES

Brie and Camembert are the most well-known bloomy rind cheeses that can be broadly described as having a soft creamy centre with an edible rind. These cheeses typically have mellow flavours of mild to moderate intensity, varying from buttery to earthy. My go-to pairings are rich styles of CHARDONNAY or CHENIN BLANC, which have a bit of weight to match the density and creaminess of these cheeses. Alternatively, indulge in an off-dry or sweeter white wine for a tantalizing contrast with the creamy flavours.

GOATS' CHEESE

This can vary from mild, soft and creamy to deeply earthy, grassy and mouth-puckeringly tangy. The classic pairing is SAUVIGNON BLANC, which can have similar flavours (grassy, mineral) and bright citrus notes, giving an overall lift. Also consider other herby whites, such as GRÜNER VELTLINER, and for an appetizing contrast try rich, honeyed whites in dry and off-dry styles, such as those made from RIESLING and CHENIN BLANC.

WASHED-RIND CHEESES

Get ready for some serious whiff! Washed-rind cheeses, such as Reblochon, Époisses and Vacherin, have strong and pungent aromas and flavours and a high fat content. Pair these cheeses with wines that can stand up to their intense umami and savoury character and cut through the fat. Sweet wines with high acidity, such as *SAUTERNES*, *TOKAJI* and RIESLING, are always winners. Rich styles of *CHAMPAGNE* are an opulent and exciting sensory match, with the prickle of bubbles and acidity providing freshness. A still CHARDONNAY in its various forms is always a delicious match – whether fresher *CHABLIS*-styles or more textured, oaked styles – as are light and fruity reds such as *BEAUJOLAIS*. With Vacherin, try pairing with wines from its cheese region in the ever-trendy Jura, which can be found in more specialist wine shops – for example, the unique, tangy and nutty Vin Jaune wines, bright mineral CHARDONNAY and SAVAGNIN (not to be confused with SAUVIGNON BLANC) and vibrant reds made from PINOT NOIR and the more unusual TROUSSEAU and POULSARD grapes.

HARD CHEESES

I find hard cheeses, such as Manchego, Cheddar, Parmesan and Comté, extremely versatile when it comes to wine pairings. These cheeses typically have deep, nutty flavours and high levels of salt and umami. My list of favourite pairings could go on and on, but here are some stellar options: fortified Sherries, from light fino styles, to the richer amontillado and woody oloroso, depending on the strength of the cheese; fortified MADEIRA wines, with their caramel nuances and electrifying acidity, as well as nutty tawny port, match superbly with a crumbly and rich cheese; aged Parmesan with SANGIOVESE and Comté with champagne are classic combinations. If in doubt, a bold and oaky CHARDONNAY will do the trick.

BLUE CHEESES

Popular blue cheeses, such as Stilton, Roquefort and Gorgonzola, typically have the strongest flavours of the cheese categories, so the bolder the wine, the better. Lusciously sweet wines, such as SAUTERNES, are always a perfect match. Another classic pairing is sweet and flavourful port, which provides a delectable sweetness to contrast with salty and tangy blues.

Best all-rounder wines with a cheese board

Many of us reach for a bottle of red when it comes to a mixed cheese board, but rich white wines and sweet wines tend to be a better fit as a result of a symmetry of flavour intensity, acidity and texture. Here are my top three wines to pair with a varied board, which are all (1) high in acidity, so will provide balance with the fatty content of a variety of cheeses, and (2) flavour-packed, so they won't be overwhelmed by strong cheese flavours. Believe me, you can't go wrong with these picks.

+ Sweet CHENIN BLANC
+ Off-dry RIESLING
+ Oaked CHARDONNAY

Baked camembert
paired with oaked chardonnay

If you love a cheese dish that's gooey and indulgent and a wine that's mouth-hugging yet fresh, this is the perfect pairing for you. There are few things that make me happier than baked cheese and an opulent style of CHARDONNAY. This recipe takes only moments to prepare, but always brings satisfied smiles. The wine and the cheese work well together because they both have body and intensity of rich flavours, but the CHARDONNAY also has a nice bit of acidity that cuts through the fat of the Camembert.

Serves 2–4

1 whole Camembert
1 garlic clove, cut into 8-10
    thin slivers
sprig of thyme, cut
    into 8-10 pieces (about
    1cm/¹/₂in each)
1 tablespoon honey
3 tablespoons white wine
black pepper

To serve

3 figs, quartered
toasted crispy bread

Preheat the oven to 200°C (180°C fan), 400°F, Gas Mark 6.

Place the Camembert in a small, low-sided ovenproof dish and score diagonally across the top in both directions to form a diamond pattern.

Insert the garlic slivers and the sprigs of thyme evenly across the Camembert, then drizzle over the honey and sprinkle with black pepper. Finally, pour over the CHARDONNAY.

Bake for 15-20 minutes until bubbling. Serve straight away with the figs and some toasted crispy bread.

SWEET

Sweet foods are best paired with wines that are equally sweet, as they can make dry wines taste bitter and acidic. I also like to think about the texture of a wine in relation to a dessert – I tend to pair delicate desserts with similarly textured sweet wines, and those that are richer and heavier together. If you are sticking with a dry wine, then it's best to opt for a wine with an expressively fruity character (such as certain styles of RIESLING and CHENIN BLANC). I generally avoid sweet food with dry red wines, apart from with chocolate. The flavours and tannin in red wine can overpower a dessert's flavours and textures, plus the coolness and freshness of certain desserts can particularly accentuate the bitterness of tannin – so lemon sorbet and SYRAH is a no-no for me.

FRUIT

With fruit-based desserts, consider the types of fruit used and the richness of the dessert to select a wine to match. With fresh citrus desserts, such as lemon tart, opt for light and zingier styles of sweet wine such as light, sweet styles of RIESLING, MOSCATO D'ASTI or a sweeter prosecco. With berry-fruited desserts, consider sweeter styles of rosé (forget white ZINFANDEL!) and try an off-dry Rosé d'Anjou from the LOIRE. For a chic affair, indulge in a demi-sec champagne with a simple bowl of strawberries and cream. With orchard fruit and tropical fruit desserts, such as poached pears, apple tart or a pineapple upside-down cake, a rich sweet RIESLING will work a treat, or a sweet CHENIN BLANC, such as those from VOUVRAY or COTEAUX DU LAYON in the LOIRE.

CREAMY

Go big or go home! I like to pair boldly flavoured desserts with something opulent and indulgent to match. Think tiramisu or cheesecake with rich fortified wines, such as the French speciality Vins Doux Naturels, or pair vanilla ice cream with PX sherry. With creamy, sweet desserts, such as crème caramel or crème brûlée, you could pick a smooth tawny port because of its similar toffee and nutty flavours. You can always rely on the rich sweet wines of SAUTERNES, TOKAJ and the sweetest styles of RIESLING and CHENIN BLANC for these desserts too.

CAKES AND PASTRIES

The classic pairing with afternoon tea cakes and pastries is champagne. It's a fresh, decadent and glamorous match – but on a taste test you might actually prefer something a little sweeter. If you fancy sticking with fizz and something dry, then I suggest picking rosé bubbles over white, as they usually have a bit more fruit flavour, which complements sweet and fruity baked goods. Sweeter bubbles (like my suggestion with strawberries and cream, opposite) are a beautiful option, but for something different and still, you could try off-dry to sweeter styles of PINOT GRIS, GEWÜRZTRAMINER or RIESLING; these wines can display gorgeous perfumed, floral and honeyed notes, which are a real joy with afternoon tea delights.

RICH AND CHOCOLATEY

With chocolatey desserts, consider whether they are based on white, milk or dark chocolate for the right wine pick. White chocolate desserts work well with sweet white and rosé styles, whereas dark chocolate is best paired with reds. Port is a classic pairing with rich, darker chocolate recipes, or even a box of luxurious chocolate truffles. Rich and fruity styles of dry red can work with chocolate – I have been known to indulge from time to time in a bar of milk chocolate with nuts and raisins paired with a juicy New World SHIRAZ or a fruity BEAUJOLAIS.

Vanilla ice-cream
paired with PX

Commonly known as PX, **PEDRO XIMÉNEZ** sherry is a lusciously
sweet, fortified wine with mouth-enveloping notes of dried figs,
dates and walnuts. I absolutely love serving a generous drizzle
of it over vanilla ice cream: a simple yet truly decadent and
indulgent treat.

Chocolate board
paired with port

A stylish chocolate board with a glass of port is something a bit different and fun to serve at the end of a meal or dinner party, on a cosy afternoon during the festive season, or just as a treat in front of the television. This board would work with all the key styles of port: ruby, late bottled vintage, vintage and tawny.

Ideas for chocolate boards:
+ Mixture of milk and dark chocolate
+ Biscotti or cantucci
+ Dried fruit, such as dates, cranberries or cherries
+ Nuts, such as walnuts, pecans and Brazil nuts
+ Fresh red-fruit berries, such as raspberries and cherries, to add colour

FLAVOURS FROM AROUND THE WORLD

In today's world, we are fortunate to be able to discover, explore and taste a plethora of cuisines from near and far without stepping foot on a plane. Books, television and social media give us access to food cultures, chefs and home cooks from across the planet, while many large cities have a diverse culinary offering in terms of restaurants.

This section of the book introduces a number of popular international cuisines alongside wine-pairing considerations and ideas. An in-depth focus on specific cuisines is beyond the scope of this book, but use these high-level introductions to help and inspire your wine choices.

CLASSIC FRENCH
Elegant ✦ Rich ✦ Balanced

Classic French cuisine is rich yet refined, with precise techniques and high-quality ingredients delivering harmonious dishes that are both comforting and poised.

Key ingredients
Garlic; shallots; butter; cream; cheese; wine; eggs; mushrooms; mustard; herbs, such as parsley and tarragon.

Wine considerations
✦ **Flavour:** From deep and mellow, such as garlic butter, to rich and fruity, such as a red wine sauce. Pair with wines of equal intensity to complement the different cooking techniques and sauces – perhaps a subtly oaked white with fish in a creamy sauce, and velvety reds with wine sauces.

✦ **Texture:** Think about the ingredients used, how they've been cooked and the resulting textures of the dish. Consider complementary textures, such as a buttery dish with a buttery white wine, or grippy braised meat with a tannic red wine.

✦ **Fat:** Dishes with a high fat element from ingredients such as butter, cream and cheese will be lifted by wines with high acidity, such as SAUVIGNON BLANC for white or PINOT NOIR for red.

Pairing ideas
Sole meunière with rich and textured whites, such as an oaked CHARDONNAY.

Quiche Lorraine with fresh and vibrant whites, such as a SAUVIGNON BLANC.

Coq au vin with fruity and savoury reds, such as a structured style of BEAUJOLAIS (Villages or Cru).

MEDITERRANEAN
Flavourful ✦ Rustic ✦ Wholesome

Mediterranean cuisine is characterized by fresh ingredients and a nourishing, hearty and convivial approach to food that unites a diverse selection of countries hugging the Mediterranean Sea.

Key ingredients
Olive oil; garlic; lemon; olives; Mediterranean herbs, such as rosemary and thyme; fresh cheeses; nightshade vegetables, such as tomatoes, aubergine (eggplant) and bell peppers; grains and legumes.

Wine considerations
✦ **Flavour**: Mediterranean cuisine is defined by bold flavours, so pair wines with similar intensity, as more nuanced and delicate wines may be overpowered. Think about highlighting specific ingredients through your wine choice, such as lemon in citrusy whites, or olive and herbs in reds, such as SYRAH/SHIRAZ.

✦ **Acidity:** Commonly used ingredients in this cuisine, such as tomato and lemon, are high in acidity, which brings out the character and flavours in easy-drinking wines. So simple, fresh and fruity wines, such as rosé and unoaked whites and reds, can be elevated when paired with this cuisine.

Pairing ideas
Classic Margherita pizza with Italian traditional-method sparkling wines, rosé, or fresh reds, such as FRAPPATO.

Moussaka with bold and rich reds, such as AGLIANICO, SYRAH/SHIRAZ or CABERNET SAUVIGNON.

Seafood paella with rich or aromatic whites, such as oaked white *RIOJA* or VIOGNIER.

SCANDINAVIAN
Fresh ✦ Simple ✦ Seasonal

Scandinavian cuisine embraces seasonal delicacies, the art of foraging, and natural, fresh and pure ingredients, punctuated by delicate nuances of pickle, herb and sweet-and-sour flavours.

Key ingredients

Root vegetables; potatoes; berries; mushrooms, such as chanterelles and ceps; peas; dill and anise; pickles; rye bread; freshwater fish; game.

Wine considerations

✦ **Flavours:** Carefully consider the intensity of flavours in this cuisine. Many dishes have delicate nuances, so are best paired with fresh, restrained wines that don't overpower the ingredients. Naturally richer-flavoured produce, such as game, can stand up to more complex and intense wines.

✦ **Texture:** Ingredients such as potatoes and rye bread have a relatively dense and stodgy texture, so pair with lighter textured wines for a satisfying balance.

✦ **Umami:** Produce such as mushrooms and game have a strong umami character, which can make wines taste bitter. The incorporation of berries and salt in Scandinavian dishes balances umami and makes the dishes more wine-friendly – but also consider fruity wines to complement umami-forward plates.

Pairing ideas

Gravlax with refreshing whites, such as MUSCADET, or bright, non-vintage CHAMPAGNE.

Swedish meatballs with flavourful, fresh reds, such as SANGIOVESE, or a structured BEAUJOLAIS.

Pork and mushroom sauce with rich whites, such as oaked CHENIN BLANC, or earthy reds, such as PINOT NOIR.

MEXICAN

Adventurous ✦ Fiery ✦ Gratifying

Mexican cuisine combines soothing and lively flavours and textures for a scintillating experience, from comforting ingredients, such as beans and corn, to the daring, with bold spices and zesty sauces.

Key ingredients

Corn; beans; vibrant vegetables; tomatoes; avocado; chillies; limes; zesty and earthy spices.

Wine considerations

✦ **Flavour:** Pair fresh and zesty dishes with similar wines, such as unoaked Italian whites. For punchier, richer-flavoured dishes, pair with bolder wine, such as an oaked CHARDONNAY or an aromatic RIESLING, or with flavourful medium- to full-bodied reds, such as MERLOT.

✦ **Spice:** Consider the spices in a dish – are they providing strong aromatics or heat? Pair with wines that can stand up to flavourful spices and be mindful of pairing high-alcohol wines with chilli heat.

✦ **Acid:** High-acid ingredients, such as lime juice and tomatoes, work well with fresh and simple wines, bringing out their personality and flavours – so consider easy-drinking fresh whites in these cases.

Pairing ideas
Enchiladas with fruity and high-acid whites and reds (depending on the filling) for lift and contrast.

Aguachile (spicy Mexican ceviche) with herby or zingy whites, such as GRÜNER VELTLINER or ALBARIÑO.

Cochinita pibil (slow-cooked pork) with smooth and spicy reds, such as a GSM blend.

MIDDLE EASTERN
Fragrant ✦ Colourful ✦ Soulful

The Middle East spans a range of people, traditions and cultures, and its cuisine centres around fragrant, floral, citrusy, aromatic and earthy spices and fare to create dynamic and hearty dishes.

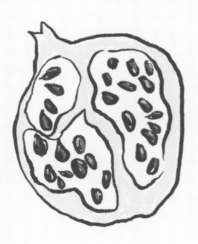

Key ingredients
Olive oil; lemon; spices, such as cumin, cardamom and saffron; fresh herbs, such as mint and parsley; tahini; grains; legumes and rice; nuts; fruits, such as pomegranate and orange; yogurt and fresh cheese.

Wine considerations
✦ **Flavours:** Vary from fresh and vibrant to savoury and earthy. If just one dish is being served, consider a matching wine that picks up on similar flavours. If a meal comprises several diverse dishes, pick a versatile wine – unoaked, fruit-forward fresh wines fit the bill, such as a youthful red *CÔTES DU RHÔNE*, a ripe ALBARIÑO and deeper-hued, dry rosés.

✦ **Spices:** Many are intense and fragrant as opposed to having heat, so pair with wines that have fragrant notes, such as SYRAH, GEWÜRZTRAMINER and orange wines.

✦ **Sweet:** Dishes often incorporate fresh, dried and cooked fruits, which can be pleasant to pair with similar-flavoured wines – think pomegranate and PINOT NOIR, or apricot and VIOGNIER.

Pairing ideas
Meat kofta, kebab or shawarma with peppery reds, such as SYRAH.

Hummus, tabbouleh and falafel with zesty whites, such as PINOT GRIGIO or SAUVIGNON BLANC.

Tagine with velvety, fruity reds, such as *RIOJA* Crianza or PRIMITIVO, orange wines and rich, aromatic whites.

INDIAN
Spicy ✦ Hearty ✦ Robust

Indian cuisine embraces a spectrum of complex spices. Recipes incorporate bold, rich and buttery flavours and textures, and meals may include a variety of cooking methods, techniques and dishes.

Key ingredients
Spices and herbs, such as garam masala, coriander and rose; root vegetables, leafy greens, pulses; tomatoes; yogurt; chutneys and pickles; rice; buttery and spiced breads.

Wine considerations
✦ **Flavours:** Intensity is the key consideration here – pair wines with the fruit intensity to stand up to bold flavours, such as New World reds, and rich whites, such as certain CHENIN BLANCS and VIOGNIERS.

✦ **Spice:** Bear in mind the level of heat used in a dish. With moderate to high heat, consider lower alcohol, fruitier and off-dry wines; with extra hot dishes, avoid wine.

✦ **Textures:** Pair a creamy or buttery curry with similarly textured wines, such as a velvety MERLOT or a buttery CHARDONNAY.

Pairing ideas
Rogan Josh (mild) with rich and full-bodied reds, such as MALBEC or *RIOJA*.

Biryani (moderately spiced) with rich and textured whites, such as VIOGNIER or white *RHÔNE* blends.

Goan fish curry (spicy) with off-dry, aromatic RIESLING – but if very hot, pour a beer.

CHINESE
Aromatic ✦ Bold ✦ Harmonious

Chinese cuisine is a symphony of layered flavours and textures. Medicinal principles, aesthetic appreciation and equilibrium inspire nourishing, colourful and flavourful dishes.

Key ingredients
Sichuan peppercorns; sesame; soy sauce; ginger; garlic; five-spice; tofu; crunchy vegetables, such as pak choi, water chestnuts and bamboo shoots; mushrooms; rice; noodles.

Wine considerations

✦ **Flavours:** Consider the intensity of flavour and the cooking techniques used. Delicately flavoured steamed dishes can pair with wines with similar qualities, whereas more robust flavours, such as five-spice and fried dishes, can be matched with bolder wines.

✦ **Spice:** Consider spices versus heat – Sichuan pepper is not usually hot, but it is a dominant flavour, so pair it with wines that have a similar pepperiness, such as SYRAH.

✦ **Umami:** Recipes that include tofu, seafood and mushrooms are umami-rich, so benefit from being paired with fruitier styles of wine and those with high acidity to lift the savouriness.

Pairing ideas

Steamed dim sum with dry, crisp sparkling wines, such as cava, or other traditional-method sparkling wines.

Sichuan beef with rich or peppery reds, such as RHÔNE-style SYRAH.

Steamed fish with ginger and shallots goes with aromatic, zesty whites, such as SAUVIGNON BLANC.

JAPANESE
Balanced ✦ Delicate ✦ Umami

Japanese cuisine values preparation and balance of the key food elements: acidity, heat, fat, salt and umami to create decorative fare, ranging from pure and nuanced to complex and rich.

Key ingredients

Seaweed; soy products; miso; wasabi; yuzu; bonito flakes (dried tuna flakes); seven-spice; rice vinegar; sesame; rice; noodles; and broths.

Wine considerations

✦ **Flavour:** Are the flavours fresh, like that of sashimi, or rich, like unagi don (grilled glazed eel)? Match intensity of flavours for balance – for example, pair raw fish with delicate CHABLIS styles of CHARDONNAY, or richer dishes with riper or oaked styles of CHARDONNAY.

✦ **Umami:** Complement umami-rich dishes (broths, eggs, shiitake, seaweed, bonito flakes) with juicy and fresh wines to brighten the savoury component, such as a fruity style of PINOT NOIR.

✦ **Variety:** Japanese meals often involve a range of plates, so consider picking a versatile wine – for example, a richer, traditional-method sparkling wine pairs well with both light and bolder dishes.

Pairing ideas

Sushi with unoaked whites, such as CHABLIS, or traditional-method sparkling wines.

Ramen with fruity, fresh reds or textured whites, such as PINOT NOIR or off-dry RIESLING.

Katsu curry with rich whites with acidity, such as CHENIN BLANC, or rosé/sparkling rosé.

KOREAN
Flavour-packed ✦ Fermented ✦ Spicy

Korean cuisine is hearty and packed with bold flavours and mouth-popping spices. Fermented ingredients and the art of preparing them play an important cultural, health and culinary role.

Key ingredients
Gochujang (red chilli paste); kimchi; fermented pastes; seaweed; sesame oil and sesame seeds; soy sauce; red bell pepper; noodles; rice.

Wine considerations
✦ **Flavours:** Be mindful of the strong flavours in this cuisine, which might overpower delicate wines. Pick wines with rich flavours, such as ripe and juicy New World styles of red and white wine.

✦ **Spice:** Many dishes are packed with chilli heat, so consider wines that have a good concentration of fruit flavour or are off-dry. Wines that are slightly lower in alcohol, such as an off-dry German RIESLING, will feel more balanced against the heat.

✦ **Umami:** Fermented flavours from kimchi and other ingredients and pastes often have savoury, tangy and pungent flavours that work well with orange wines and rich and spicy whites, such as VIOGNIER.

Pairing ideas
Bibimbap with fresh, aromatic, off-dry whites, such as RIESLING or PINOT GRIS, or juicy reds.

Fried chicken with traditional-method sparkling wines, or white or rosé wines with high acidity.

Korean barbecue with medium- to full-bodied red wines, such as structured BEAUJOLAIS, SYRAH and MALBEC.

THAI
Vibrant ✦ Aromatic ✦ Spicy

Thai cuisine centres around fresh and bold ingredients presented in a variety of ways – curry, salad, barbecue, soup – that carefully balance spicy, sweet, salty, sour and nutty elements.

Key ingredients
Fish sauce; bird's eye chilli; palm sugar; lime juice; coconut milk; herbs, such as lemongrass, Thai basil and makrut lime leaves; rice; noodles; curry pastes.

Wine considerations

✦ **Flavour:** Many dishes have strong flavours – zesty, herby, earthy or nutty – which can overpower delicate wines. Avoid nuanced fine wines that may get lost in the flavours, and pair with simple and fresh wines for a laid-back experience (such as easy-drinking PINOT GRIGIO), or wines with an aromatic or bold character (such as RIESLING or MERLOT) to balance intense flavours.

✦ **Spice:** There are many fiery dishes in Thai cuisine, and off-dry whites work particularly well with chilli heat. But once heat turns seriously hot, a wine's flavour will be lost, in which case, pick a refreshing beer or juice instead.

Pairing ideas

Pad Thai (mildly spiced) with flavourful, rich whites, such as an Alsatian PINOT GRIS.

Massaman curry (rich and moderately spiced) with bold and smooth reds, such as a PRIMITIVO.

Green curry (spicy) with off-dry RIESLING or CHENIN BLANC – but if the curry is very hot, open a beer.

VIETNAMESE
Aromatic ✦ Fresh ✦ Balanced

Vietnamese cuisine nourishes the soul with its warming broths, crunchy salads and satisfying staples. It uses an abundance of fresh, aromatic herbs and colour, while carefully balancing the key tastes.

Key ingredients

Fresh herbs, such as coriander and mint; lemongrass; lime; fish sauce; garlic; ginger; shallots; shrimp paste; broth variations; rice; rice noodles.

Wine considerations

✦ **Flavours:** Dishes based on fresh, bright and vibrant herbs and citrus pair well with mineral-driven, lemony whites, such as SAUVIGNON BLANC or ALBARIÑO. Match meatier dishes with earthy, smoky flavours, or sweeter marinated-meat dishes with fruity and fresh reds or honeyed whites, such as CHENIN BLANC.

✦ **Spice:** Generally Vietnamese cuisine is not as hot as neighbouring Thai cuisine, but with spicy dishes avoid high-alcohol, tannic reds and opt for fruitier or off-dry styles of red and white.

✦ **Umami:** pho-style broths are rich in umami so suit being paired with light and fruity styles of red, such as PINOT NOIR, or fresh, flavourful whites, such as CHENIN BLANC, or off-dry whites, such as RIESLING.

Pairing ideas

Beef pho (noodle soup) with fruit-forward and fresh reds, such as BEAUJOLAIS.

Grilled caramelized pork and vermicelli with rich or off-dry CHENIN BLANC or PINOT GRIS, or fruity reds.

Fresh prawn spring rolls with herby, citrusy whites, such as SAUVIGNON BLANC or GRÜNER VELTLINER.

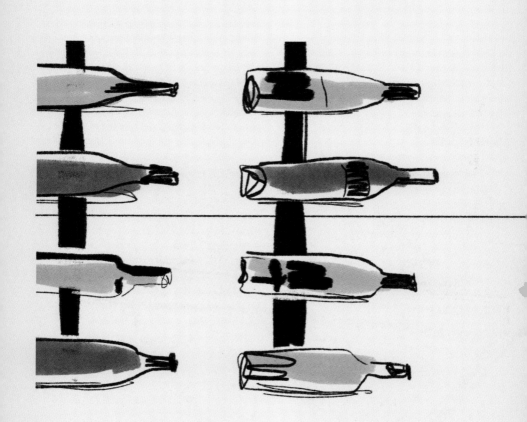

WINE
AT
HOME

HOW TO READ A WINE LABEL

We've all found ourselves standing in the wine aisle or scrolling online confronted by a vast selection of bottles and feeling overwhelmed by both mystery and choice. So many different labels, some traditional, others minimalist and some adorned with striking artwork. On closer inspection, some bottles of wine have lots of information on the front or back label, making life a bit easier, and others virtually nothing (not even a back label). Ultimately, you just want to know what's in the bottle and how it will taste so you can decide whether to buy it. I understand – let's unpack and break down the information on a wine label to help your buying choices.

In most countries, certain information is required on a wine label, such as the liquid quantity, alcohol level, country of origin, government warning and allergy information. The other minimum information included will usually be dictated by the wine region and country-specific regulations based on where the wine is sold. The inclusion of any additional information, such as tasting notes or information about the vineyards and winery, will be the choice of the individual wine producer.

INFORMATION TYPICALLY INCLUDED ON A WINE LABEL

+ **Name of the producer or winery**

+ **Name of the wine or the brand:** Not all wines have a name; some might be known by the name of the producer/winery or the wine region (appellation).

+ **Wine region/appellation:** The place in which the grapes are grown and the wine is made (see opposite).

+ **Vintage:** The year in which the grapes for the wine were harvested. Note that many sparkling wines are made as 'non-vintage' wines – see page 63 for more information.

+ **Grapes:** The variety or varieties used in the wine may be shown on the label. This is more common on wine from New World countries than Old World countries.

+ **Other information:** Brief details of wine-growing and winemaking practices may be included on some labels, where you might also find a tasting note and sometimes suggested pairings.

+ **Certification:** A guarantee issued by a recognized body that a wine is what it claims to be – organic, biodynamic, sustainable, etc.

+ **Awards:** National or international awards can be found on the label or elsewhere on the bottle in the form of a stamp or sticker.

+ **QR code:** Increasingly popular, these scannable barcodes take the consumer to a website with information about the wine: grapes, vintage, tasting notes, pairings, etc.

Grapes vs. regions

One of the most puzzling aspects of wine is knowing how to tell the difference between grapes and wine regions. The confusion can arise when looking at labels, and in the way that people commonly refer to and talk about different wines. Some wine labels will state only the wine region and not the grape variety/varieties.

Why do wine regions do this? It's wrapped up in long-standing laws and traditions in many wine regions, where over time they have built their reputation and specific style based on the significance of the place they are from. Below are some examples of wines labelled and commonly referred to by the wine region instead of the grape:

+ *CHABLIS* or white *BURGUNDY* (the grape is CHARDONNAY)
+ *SANCERRE* (the grape is SAUVIGNON BLANC)
+ *CHIANTI* (the key grape is SANGIOVESE)
+ *BAROLO* (the grape is NEBBIOLO)
+ red *RIOJA* (the key grape is TEMPRANILLO)

Navigating a Wine Label

Name of the producer or the winery: Louis Jadot

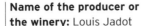

Vintage: 2022

Country of origin: France

VIN DE BOURGOGNE

CELLIER DU VALVAN

CHABLIS

Appellation d'Origine Contrôlée

Mis en bouteilles à F 71570-090 par

LOUIS JADOT

BEAUNE - FRANCE

PRODUCT OF FRANCE

75 CL - 12,5% Vol.

CONTAINS SULPHITES

Imported by: Hatch Mansfield, New Bank House
1 Brockenhurst Road, Ascot, Berkshire, SL5 9DJ-UK
www.hatchmansfield.com

Alcohol level: 12.5%

Name of the wine or the brand: Cellier du Valvan

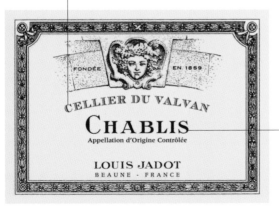

Wine region/appellation: *CHABLIS*
Note that just the region is on the label and not the grape variety, which is common in European labelling. The only grape permitted in *CHABLIS* is the white grape **CHARDONNAY**.

Name of the producer or the winery: Penfolds

Penfolds

KOONUNGA HILL

SHIRAZ

FIRST VINTAGE 2002

PENFOLDS WINES SOUTH AUSTRALIA

ESTABLISHED 1844

2021

Name of the wine or the brand: Koonunga Hill

Vintage: 2021

Grape: SHIRAZ. Note that, unlike the CHABLIS label opposite, the grape variety here is included on the label.

Wine region/appellation: South Australia

Penfolds

KOONUNGA HILL

SHIRAZ

2021

Opulent red Shiraz fruits are beautifully captured in this vibrant, multi-regional blend. Subtle oak, balanced acidity and fine tannins frame an impressive palate. Koonunga Hill wines are known for their generosity of flavour, balance and lasting quality.

PENFOLDS WINES ESTABLISHED 1844

PENFOLDS WINES PTY LTD 78 PENFOLD ROAD MAGILL SA 5072 AUSTRALIA
CONTAINS SULPHITES 14.5% ALC/VOL · PRODUCED WITH THE AID OF EGG
AND MILK PRODUCTS AND TRACES MAY REMAIN
WINE OF AUSTRALIA
www.penfolds.com
CONSUMER INFORMATION
AUST 1300 651 650 · NZ 0800 651 650
For calorie information see -
www.penfolds.com/calories

750 mL

Standard Drinks 8.6

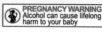

PREGNANCY WARNING Alcohol can cause lifelong harm to your baby

Other information: Tasting notes on the label on the back of the bottle.

Alcohol level: 14.5%

Country of origin: Australia

WHAT IS A WINE APPELLATION?

A wine appellation is a legally defined geographical area governed by a body that sets outs specific rules and regulations about grape-growing and winemaking practices. Producers seeking to put an appellation on their label usually apply to their specific regional body and may be subject to certain inspections, tastings and information disclosures before they are approved. When you see the name of the appellation or its stamp on the bottle it guarantees that the wine has been made in accordance with the requirements of that place.

Appellation rules may regulate the type of grapes that can be used in the wine – for example, the appellation of CHABLIS permits the use of only the white grape CHARDONNAY. There may be very specific requirements about the alcohol level, style of wine, oak use and ageing – for example, the wines of CHIANTI and RIOJA have certain minimum oak-barrel and bottle-age requirements. The appellation rules may also cover many other provisions required in the vineyard and the winery. When picking a wine, understanding the appellation is a useful indicator of the grapes, style and taste of a wine if there is little information available on the label, or when you are narrowing down your selection from a wine list.

Appellations vary in size – they can be country-wide, regional or subregional; they can cover a town, a village, a vineyard, or even just a few select rows of vines in certain famed vineyards. Their boundaries may be based on specific geological or geographical features that make the resulting wines unique. Usually, the larger the geographical appellation, the more relaxed the regulations and the simpler the wines; whereas the smaller the appellation, the stricter the requirements and the higher the quality of the wines. As is always the case with wine, there are exceptions – but this is generally a good starting point.

Let's look at France and the region of BURGUNDY to illustrate the widest to the smallest size of appellation:

Country: France
Region: Burgundy
Subregion: Côte de Nuits
Village: Gevrey-Chambertin
Vineyard: Le Chambertin.

WHERE TO BUY WINE

✦ Supermarket/grocery store: These outlets often stock wines starting at entry-level price points from international brands through to mid- and premium-priced wines, depending on the store and size, though they tend to focus on value, easy-drinking wines. Many work with large wine producers to create own-label wines, which are typically of sound quality and affordably priced.

✦ Wine retailers: Large specialist retailers have a broad selection of wines from a range of regions and across various price points, typically with more diverse and premium labels than a supermarket/grocery store. Small retailers may have a more curated selection of wines, and may specialize in certain regions or styles, or in fine wines. Often experienced specialists work in the shops and will offer advice to customers. Some wine retailers create own-label bottlings with producers they work with, which are usually reliable, good-quality and well-priced options.

✦ Online: Many wine shops are now online-only. They may have a small range or a vast selection of wines, or areas of specialist expertise. There's no limit to what you can find online, from entry-level to rare, unusual and fine wines.

HOW MUCH TO SPEND ON A BOTTLE OF WINE

Aside from the portion of the price attributable to the wine itself, there are numerous direct and indirect costs that add up to the total price of the bottle. In many markets across the world, in the entry- to mid-level price bracket, it can be disheartening to know how small a proportion of the price goes towards the actual wine relative to the ancillary costs. Let's take the UK for example, and an entry-level bottle of wine costing £5.50: the value of the wine in the bottle can be as low as 20 pence, with the remaining £5.30 covering packaging, logistics, duty, tax and supplier/retailer profit margins.

However, as many of these costs are fixed, when you spend a bit more on a bottle, a larger proportion of that money should go towards the actual wine. For example, with a bottle priced at £10, the value of the wine itself increases to £2.50, about ten times that of the £5.50 bottle.*

When it comes to what to spend on a bottle of wine, my advice is to avoid buying the cheapest bulk wines. Although it is not always the case, the reality is that to produce many wines at such a low cost

*Figures shared with permission from Bibendum's *Vinonomics* report, March 2023.
https://www.bibendum-wine.co.uk/news-stories/articles/wine/uk-wine-duty-explained-vinonomics/

means that compromises are likely to have been made during the production process at the expense of the environment, the labour force involved, or the quality of the wine.

The price of a bottle is also affected by factors including the land, labour and production costs in a particular region or country, currency conversion rates for imported/exported wine, and the regional reputation, brand and marketing costs. These factors should all be considered when purchasing a bottle.

TIPS FOR BUYING WINE AND FINDING VALUE

✦ Generally, the smaller the wine appellation, the better the quality of the wine: For example, a wine labelled as specifically from *NAPA VALLEY* in *CALIFORNIA* is likely to be better quality than a wine labelled just '*CALIFORNIA*'; the same applies to *PAUILLAC* in *BORDEAUX* compared to just '*BORDEAUX*'. Wine appellations that cover large geographical areas are likely to contain grapes that have been broadly sourced, which can be of varying quality and tend to be subject to less rigorous growing and production rules.

✦ Experiment with lesser-known regions: Central and Eastern Europe have a long history of winemaking and offer delicious wines from native and international grapes at excellent value. I'm particularly excited by wines from Romania, Hungary and Bulgaria. If you're a fan of Provence-style rosés without the price tag, check out those from the neighbouring *LANGUEDOC*, or from *NAVARRA* in Spain. South America also offers great value: put Uruguay on your radar; check out the exciting, fresh *CHARDONNAY* from *LIMARÍ* in Chile; and try classic white and red wines from the *UCO VALLEY* (subregion of *MENDOZA*) in Argentina.

＋ Look out for underrated grapes:
CHENIN BLANC is regularly hailed as the
world's most underrated white grape.
The native Greek grapes ASSYRTIKO (white)
and XINOMAVRO (red) have been recognized
as Greece's answer to *CHABLIS* and *BAROLO*
(respectively) at affordable prices. Lovers
of crisp whites should try Spanish VERDEJO
(from *RUEDA*) or dry FURMINT from Hungary.
Fans of bold and juicy reds should try
southern Italian PRIMITIVO or Chilean
CARMENÈRE, both usually priced attractively.
South African PINOTAGE has suffered from a
mixed reputation in the past, but I say make
up your own mind, as there is an increasing
number of modern, fruity, affordable styles
made from this grape.

**＋ Be careful of being lured by pretty
labels and celebrity-owned wines:** Don't
judge a wine by its cover! Remember
to focus on what's in the bottle
and not just the marketing
strategy.

**＋ Be cautious of discounts
and sales:** There are many
reasons why a wine might be
discounted or in a sale – a brand
may have paid for the promotion,
the original price could have been
too high to begin with, the retailer
may want to ease surplus stock or
get rid of wines coming to the end of
their optimum drinking window. But sales
can also be a great way to pick up quality
wines from recognized premium brands
for less – for example, purchasing well-

known *CHAMPAGNE* brands outside the major
festive and holiday periods is a great way of
making a saving.

＋ Value wines from leading producers:
Look for great value, entry-level wines from
top producers with great reputations – for
example, Ken Forrester (South Africa),
Penfolds (Australia), Famille Perrin (France),
Antinori (Italy) and Torres (Spain).

＋ See also: Alternatives to champagne,
page 61; Impress for less: Red wines, page
206; Impress for less: White and sparkling
wines, page 210; Crowd-pleasers, page 214.

WINE CLOSURES

Cork has a long tradition as a closure in winemaking, especially in Europe, and many people enjoy the custom and ceremony of opening a bottle sealed this way.

Wines bottled under cork allow for a tiny bit of oxygen transfer, which is beneficial for some wines, allowing certain aromas, flavours and textures to develop during the ageing process. The chemical compound known by its acronym TCA is responsible for undesirable wet-cardboard (musty) smells referred to as 'cork taint', or for causing a wine to be 'corked' – this is more common in wines sealed under natural cork than other closures.

Today, many producers use synthetic corks that are more predictable and less prone to issues. A screwcap closure provides an airtight seal preventing any oxygen transfer, which can be beneficial for retaining freshness in a wine. Australia and New Zealand have been at the forefront of using screwcaps for quality wines, and they are now commonly used for wines at a range of price points across the world. There are a few common misconceptions about screwcaps: the key myths to bust are that they are used only for entry-level wines, and that they can't be used for wines to be aged. Both are not the case.

OPENING A BOTTLE OF STILL WINE

Here is how to open a bottle of wine with a type of corkscrew commonly known as a 'waiter's friend', which has a small blade for cutting the foil and a lever system for raising the cork. It is also small and foldable, so can be kept discreetly in a pocket.

Step 1: Cut the foil under the rim and remove it.

Step 2: Place a corkscrew in the middle of the cork.

Step 3: Slowly wind the corkscrew clockwise, keeping it straight.

Step 4: Place the lever on the top of the bottle and carefully pull upwards.

OPENING A BOTTLE OF SPARKLING WINE

To prevent flying corks and mass spillage on opening a bottle of sparkling wine, make sure it's chilled (see page 184), as this decreases the pressure of the bubbles, and avoid shaking the bottle. Here are the rest of the steps for a seamless experience.

Step 1: Remove the foil that covers the wire cage.

Step 2: Keep a firm hand on top of the wire cage and the cork at all times, then slowly unwind the wire cage until it is loosely sitting on top of the cork.

Step 3: Slowly twist the bottle (not the cork) until there is a gentle release of the cork.

OPENING A WINE WITH A WAX SEAL

Wax seals have gained in popularity in some regions and with some producers. But if hacked in the wrong way, these can cause a mess, with crumbling wax entering your wine. The best way to open a wine with a wax seal is to pretend it's not there. Insert the corkscrew through it and the top of the wax usually comes away in one circular piece as the cork is levered out, rather than breaking into lots of little pieces.

Step 1: Go straight through the wax with a corkscrew.

Step 2: Lever out the cork as you would when opening a bottle without a wax seal (see page 177).

GLASSWARE

There's a vast selection of glassware available, with some brands even designing glass shapes for specific grapes and regions for a heightened sensory experience. It can be hard to know where to start and what to buy, so here I'm sharing my top tips to suit a variety of budgets, occasions and available storage space.

WHITE WINE

White wine glasses usually have a medium-sized bowl and a gently angled rim that tapers inwards. Full-bodied, rich styles of white wine, such as oaked CHARDONNAY, can benefit from being served in a wider bowl-shaped glass.

RED WINE

Red wine glasses are the largest-sized wine glass, with a medium-to-large bowl and a gently angled rim tapering inwards. Full-bodied reds, such as CABERNET SAUVIGNON, can benefit from being served in large, tall glasses, whereas delicate, perfumed red wines, such as PINOT NOIR, can benefit from being served in wider bowl-shaped glasses.

UNIVERSAL

I love a one-size-fits-all glass, made to suit wines from sparkling to sweet and ideal when storage space is tight. Universal glasses made by high-quality brands can be expensive, but many medium-sized red wine glasses will fit the bill. The key features are:

✦ **Long stem:** So the glass can be held by the stem (not the bowl) to prevent the wine warming from contact with the hands.

✦ **Medium-sized bowl:** To allow the wine to be swirled around, and for aromas and flavours to be gently released.

✦ **Gently angled rim:** To keep the aromas and flavours concentrated in the glass.

STEMLESS

Perhaps surprisingly, I really like stemless glasses for certain occasions. The main criticism of these glasses is that holding the bowl warms the wine, resulting in a loss of freshness. But when serving easy-drinking wines in informal settings, these are a great option. They are far less fragile, resulting in fewer breakages, and perfect if you're at a picnic or outdoor event. Look for a wide bowl and a thin rim that angles inwards.

SPARKLING WINE

Flutes have traditionally been the most popular style of glass for sparkling wine. However, in recent years there has been a move towards serving bubbles in wine glasses with a larger bowl so that the bouquet can be fully enjoyed. If you like flutes, keep them for easy-drinking sparkling wine and fresh, non-vintage champagne. For full aromatic appreciation, I would suggest using a more traditional wine glass for richer, gastronomic sparkling wine and vintage champagne.

SWEET AND FORTIFIED

Sweet and fortified wines are usually served in a small glass, as the pour is smaller, given the sweetness or high-alcohol level.

How much wine to pour in a glass?

A good general rule is to pour to the widest part of the wine glass. For more traditional-style flutes, aim to fill between half to two-thirds of the glass.

DECANTING

PURPOSE

Decanters looks great and make lovely gifts, but what's their actual purpose? Their two main functions are to:

+ **Aerate a wine:** To allow a wine's aromas and flavours to be released as they are brought into contact with oxygen. This may give the effect of softening high tannins in red wines, as high tannins may feel more balanced once aromas and flavours are enhanced.

+ **Separate the sediment from a wine:** Carefully pouring the wine from the bottle into the decanter ensures that any sediment remains in the bottle or is trapped in the curve of the bottle neck.

WHEN TO DECANT

Different people and establishments have varying approaches to decanting wine. This is my general approach:

+ **Red wines:** Consider decanting young, bold, heavily oaked and tannic red wines (those made from grape varieties such as CABERNET SAUVIGNON and NEBBIOLO) an hour before you plan to drink the wines. I don't generally decant delicate reds (such as PINOT NOIR), and I am careful about decanting older wines as this can disrupt their aromas, flavours and texture – instead I will pour these wines into a glass for a moment before drinking, or use a glass with a large bowl for more oxygen contact.

+ **White wines:** I don't usually decant white wines, but there is an argument for decanting full-bodied, rich and oaked styles of white wine (a VIOGNIER or an oaked CHARDONNAY, for example) to allow their aromas and flavours to open fully. Alternatively, as suggested for delicate red wines, you can consider pouring these styles of white into a glass for a moment to open up before drinking, or serve them in a glass with a large bowl for increased oxygen contact.

SERVING TEMPERATURE

There's nothing worse than bringing a glass of white to your lips, anticipating the freshness of that wine, only to be wholly disappointed by taking a lukewarm sip that leaves you feeling unsatisfied and a bit sad. While I am relaxed about many aspects of wine, I will confess that I am fussy when it comes to serving temperature. Experimenting and serving wines at the temperature you enjoy is key to complementing their aromas, flavours and textures, and your overall experience. The two most common issues I see are serving white wines too cold and red wines too warm.

+ If a white wine is served ice cold, it masks aromas and flavours and can make the wine seem dull, thin and acidic. White wines are usually best served between 7–12°C (45–50°F), depending on the style.

+ If a red wine is served too warm, it will lose its freshness and vibrancy and can taste a bit flat. Room temperature (around 21°C/70°F) is generally too warm to serve red wines, which are usually best served between 12–18°C (54–64°F), depending on the style.

HOW TO PREPARE

Here is my guide to getting a wine to an attractive temperature if the bottle is currently at room temperature. Bear in mind that fridges work differently, room temperatures vary, and that there is, of course, an element of personal preference – this is a guide, not gospel.

+ **Sparkling wines:** Chill in the fridge for 2 hours, then serve immediately.

+ **Sweet wines:** Chill in the fridge for 2 hours, then serve immediately.

+ **Light- to medium-bodied white wines:** Chill in the fridge for 1$\frac{1}{2}$ hours, then serve immediately.

+ **Full-bodied and oaked white wines:** Chill in the fridge for 1 hour, then remove and open 15 minutes before serving.

+ **Rosé wines:** Chill in the fridge for 1$\frac{1}{2}$ hours, then serve immediately.

+ **Light- to medium-bodied red wines:** Chill in the fridge for 45 minutes, then remove and open 15 minutes before serving.

+ Full-bodied red wines: Chill in the fridge for 30 minutes, then remove and open 30 minutes before serving.

+ Orange wines: Chill in the fridge for 45 minutes, then remove and open 15 minutes before serving.

+ Fortified wines: Treat light-bodied and light-coloured styles (such as fino sherry) like a light- to medium-bodied white; treat deeper coloured, medium- to full-bodied styles (a vintage port, for example) like a the equivalent style of red.

Caution with quick fixes!

+ Sparkling wine in the freezer: I've seen too many people forget about wines they've left in the freezer...it can affect the integrity of the wine or may cause bottles to explode.

+ Adding ice cubes to a glass of white or rosé: I know it's tempting on a hot day but adding ice to a wine can quickly dilute its lovely aromas and flavours. Put the bottle in an ice bucket, where it will cool in under ten minutes, or in the fridge – I promise it will taste much better. If ice cubes must be used, add to simple, easy-drinking whites or rosés.

+ Heating red wine on the radiator: Again, this can affect the quality of a wine or cause it to warm unevenly. It's much better to allow a red to warm slowly at room temperature.

MY TOP WINE GADGETS AND ACCESSORIES

1. Waiter's friend: A classic and reliable bottle opener.

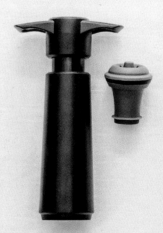

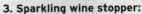

2. Coravin™: An investment piece that allows you to sample wine from a bottle without opening it, via a thin needle that extracts wine through the cork and pumps in argon gas to preserve the wine.

3. Sparkling wine stopper: A simple tool to retain the bubbles in an opened bottle of sparkling wine. Myth bust: a spoon placed handle-down in the neck of the bottle will not save your bubbles.

4. Vacuum pump: A simple and affordable system that preserves wines for several days after opening – pump out the air and pop the resealed bottle in the fridge.

5. Ice bucket: Handy for chilling a wine, and it looks great too.

STORING AND AGEING WINE

Wine is alive! Its aromas, flavours and texture change and evolve over time, which is one of the most magical and fascinating things about it. But it's a common misconception that all wines get better with age. In fact, the vast majority of wines are not meant to be aged for a long time and should be drunk within a couple of years of release.

Only a tiny proportion of wines benefit from an extended ageing process. A wine that has been aged for too long will begin to lose its aromas, flavours and freshness, and will taste muted and stale.

Wines that are suitable for ageing commonly share a few characteristics that allow them to develop positively over time. Broadly speaking, they need a concentration of aromas and flavours in their youth, and to have certain structural components that assist ageing and act as a preservative, namely tannins (for red wines) and high acidity. There are also several other factors that can affect how long a wine can positively age, including the particular grape variety or varieties used, the vintage and how that affected the grapes that year, and the winemaking processes employed.

CONDITIONS FOR STORING WINE

Wines for ageing and long-term storage should be kept in specific conditions to preserve the bottles. My approach is to try, as far as possible, to adopt the following practices for all wines kept at home (not only my special ones), to get the very best out of every bottle.

+ Store at a cool, consistent temperature: Between 10–15°C (50–59°F) is recommended, but note that wines are usually more sensitive to temperatures that are too warm than too cold. A wine fridge is a great investment and can usually be set to a specific temperature. A budget-friendly alternative is to find the coolest part of your home, for example a cupboard away from radiators, the boiler or the oven. Wines for more immediate consumption can also be stored in the fridge.

+ Store away from vibrations or movement: These can affect a wine, so avoid storing bottles above your washing machine. If you have a wine fridge in your kitchen, think about where best to place it and if any appliances nearby might cause unwanted movement.

+ Store away from light: UV rays and artificial light can damage wine. Some wine fridges have tinted glass, which takes care of this issue; otherwise find a dark spot in your home.

+ Store on the side if sealed by cork:
If a wine sealed with a cork is stored upright, it can cause the cork to dry out, as it's no longer in contact with the wine. This can lead to oxidation and spoilage. You don't need to worry about storing screwcap wines in this way.

Wine bottle sizes

A standard wine bottle is 750ml, but bottles are available in a range of sizes. Small formats, such as a demi (375ml), are often perfect for sweet wines, where a smaller pour may be served after dinner. Magnums (1.5 litres) are great in a group dinner setting, and even larger formats can be a fitting choice at big celebratory events.

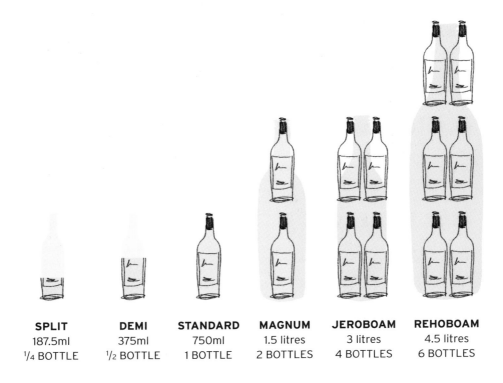

SPLIT	DEMI	STANDARD	MAGNUM	JEROBOAM	REHOBOAM
187.5ml	375ml	750ml	1.5 litres	3 litres	4.5 litres
¼ BOTTLE	½ BOTTLE	1 BOTTLE	2 BOTTLES	4 BOTTLES	6 BOTTLES

METHUSELAH
6 litres
8 BOTTLES

SALMANAZAR
9 litres
12 BOTTLES

BALTHAZAR
12 litres
16 BOTTLES

NEBUCHADNEZZAR
15 litres
20 BOTTLES

Wine bottle shapes

Most wine bottles are made from tinted glass to protect the
content from light exposure, which can affect the quality
of a wine over time. Here are some of the most recognized
bottle shapes traditionally associated with particular wine
regions. For an introduction to alternative
packaging materials for wine, see page 215.

CHIANTI
Traditional 'fiasco'
bottle, round-bottomed
flask set in a straw
basket for stability.

PORT
Dark glass to protect
wine from light, with
a bulb in the neck to
trap excess sediment
when pouring.

TOKAJI
Long-necked bottle
with a capacity of
500ml; clear glass.

BORDEAUX
Most common shape, with straight sides and high shoulders. Green or brown glass for red wines, clear for white wines.

BURGUNDY
Sloping shoulders, with longer neck than Bordeaux. Most often used for CHARDONNAY, also SAUVIGNON BLANC and PINOT NOIR.

ALSACE/ RHINE/MOSEL
Taller and thinner than Bordeaux bottle. Often green glass for German RIESLING, brown for French RIESLING.

CÔTES DE PROVENCE
Elongated hourglass shape with tapered base. Clear glass showcases the colour of the wine.

WINE
OUT AND
ABOUT

THE ROLE OF A SOMMELIER

A specialist wine waiter, known as a sommelier (or informally as a somm), specializes in looking after wine service in a restaurant. At the table, their role is to guide and advise guests on their wine list to enhance the overall dining experience.

Sommeliers may have undergone formal training and be equipped with extensive knowledge of wine and the service of wines. They may also wear a pin, often in the form of a bunch of grapes, to indicate their role, or a pin that signifies they have passed certain examinations. A sommelier may also work behind the scenes, with responsibility for buying wines, curating the wine list, managing storage, working with the chefs for a holistic food and beverage offering, and involvement in staff training. Sommeliers are found not just in fine-dining establishments, but in a range of restaurants and wine bars. Venues that don't have a sommelier may have a waiter designated to looking after wine for guests, or it may be the responsibility of the general manager.

RESTAURANT WINE ETIQUETTE

Tasting a wine in a restaurant can be one of those awkward moments, where you seem to be involved in a sort of performance but you don't have the script, so you just smile and nod enthusiastically through the whole process. What exactly are you meant to be doing? The point of this exercise is for you to check that you are drinking the wine

you ordered and that the wine is free from any flaws. In certain venues, you'll find a bit more of a show with this part of dining, but enjoy and embrace it. Wine people love to share their passion with their guests. So let's break down the typical steps for trying a wine:

+ Presentation of the wine: Once the wine has been selected, the sommelier will present the unopened bottle of wine for the guest to inspect. This is an opportunity to check the wine is exactly what was ordered, namely, the right producer, the exact wine and the correct vintage.

+ Sommelier opens and checks the wine: The sommelier will carefully open the wine, and if the bottle is sealed by cork, may check its condition. Depending on the establishment, the sommelier may pour a small amount of wine (whether sealed by cork or screwcap) into a glass to check it is free from any flaws by smelling the wine and tasting if required or typical in their venue.

+ Guest checks the wine: The sommelier will then ask if the guest who ordered the wine would like to try it, or if they wish to delegate this exercise to another guest. The reason for trying the wine is not to check whether it's nice, but to check for issues in the wine (remind yourself of these on page 18). The sommelier will pour the guest who is trying the wine a small amount to check for flaws by swirling and smelling the wine and taking a small sip (some guests will feel confident checking a wine by just smelling it, but it's perfectly acceptable to take a small sip too).

✛ **Pour for the table:** Once the wine has been checked and approved by the guest,

the sommelier may suggest that the wine is decanted or chilled before it is poured, depending on the wine. Or, if it is agreed that the wine is ready to pour, it is normal practice for the sommelier to pour wine for any other guests at the table, before coming back and topping up the guest who tried the wine. So if you were the guest who initially checked the wine, you haven't been forgotten – you'll be topped up momentarily.

....And enjoy.

TACKLING THE WINE LIST:
WHAT TO CONSIDER

You've just sat down in a restaurant or bar, and you're handed the wine list. You may have checked it out online, but chances are you're looking at it for the first time. And now it's time to make that all-important decision. Here are some handy considerations to help streamline your choices before thumbing that wine list.

You needn't waste good chatting time perusing every entry in silence. In fact, you can narrow down your selection before even taking a peek at the list.

✦ How many people are dining?
Two people may split a bottle, but if you'd like to try a couple of different of wines, see if there are any half-bottle formats and what's available by the glass. Group set-ups give more flexibility for trying different wines throughout a meal, as one bottle pours between four and five medium glasses. Magnums are a great option for groups of more than six people.

✦ What's the occasion?
Is it a casual catch-up, a business engagement, or a celebratory affair?

This may dictate the style of wine you want to drink – something easy-drinking, a fine wine, or a sparkling wine to mark an occasion. Are you meeting in the day or the evening? During the day, many people prefer to drink less and favour lighter-bodied and lower-alcohol styles.

✦ What is the budget?
This is a key consideration. It's good to approach a wine list with a price bracket or maximum amount you are willing to spend in mind. If you are splitting the bill, check the budget with your guests.

✦ What are you eating?
Think about the general cuisine of the restaurant or what you and your table are planning to eat. If you need time to consider the food options, how about ordering an apéritif while you decide? See pages 116–65 for more information on matching food and wine.

✦ What style are you in the mood for?
From the outset, think about what would really hit the spot and be enjoyable. Consider a progression in wine styles (generally from light to full-bodied, white to red) if you or your table plan to have more than one wine. Do you feel like trying something familiar, or are you up for something more experimental and unusual?

✦ What do your guests like?
Check if your guests have any wine preferences. If they don't feel confident talking about wine, you can ask them broad questions, such as if they prefer white or red wine, oaked or unoaked wines, or light or bold wines.

Restaurant etiquette: Bring your own (BYO) and corkage

- ✦ Phone or email ahead to check the restaurant's policy on BYO.
- ✦ Check the corkage fee – the amount a restaurant charges when you bring your own wine.
- ✦ Consider the bottle you are bringing; it should be something that's not already on the wine list and that's worth

paying the corkage fee on.
- ✦ Take an unopened bottle to the restaurant – the sommelier will open it but may not check the wine unless you ask them to.
- ✦ Offer the sommelier a taste of the wine.

TACKLING THE WINE LIST: MAKING A SELECTION

There isn't a standard way in which wine lists are set out: some venues structure lists by country and region, others by style (for example, light and fruity, smooth and silky, bold and robust), while some may structure under broad headings, such as white, red and sparkling. Here are my general tips for tackling wine lists.

Once you've had a moment to reflect on the initial considerations (see pages 198–9) – what I think of as the context for picking a wine – it's time to make your selection from the list.

+ **Talk to the sommelier:** Even as a wine professional, I often ask for guidance and advice from the sommelier or wine waiter. They know their wine list best and are there to enhance your overall wining and dining experience. If you're looking for a recommendation, my advice is to give your sommelier boundaries and information – tell them your budget, what style of wine you're in the mood for, something else that you like for context, and whether you're in the mood for something recognizable, or fancy something adventurous.

+ **Tackling long lists:** If you are handed a wine list of epic proportions, have no fear! Most restaurants with long lists include a 'sommelier's selection' or 'house selection' at the beginning of the list. This is a smaller range of wines designed to give a flavour of the broader wine offering, and includes popular choices that work well with the restaurant's food. Where there isn't a short

selection and you're feeling overwhelmed, revert to the first point and talk to the sommelier.

+ **Don't be snobby about the house wine:** In many wine bars and wine-orientated restaurants, careful consideration is put into selecting an approachable and tasty house wine to offer guests. Some restaurants may work in collaboration with a wine producer to make a special label for the restaurant, while others may simply offer a tried-and-tested choice that they know is popular with their guests.

+ **If a bottle is available by the glass, ask for a taste first:** Many restaurants will be happy to offer you a taste of a wine that is available by the glass before you order a bottle of that wine, to check that you like the style of a wine. Remember that when you order a bottle of wine directly from the list that isn't available by the glass, you initially taste it for faults, not to see whether you like it.

+ **Mark-ups on wines:** Depending on where you are in the world, restaurant mark-ups can be three or four times the retail price of a wine. However, you may find at the more premium end that the mark-ups aren't as substantial as this and may be formulated differently (as a fixed cash mark-up, for example, rather than a percentage), so going for something a little more expensive as a treat may also be a savvy option.

QUICK GUIDE
TO THE
PERFECT CHOICE

CLASSIC FINE RED WINES

Here are five big-hitter wine regions producing famous, fine red wines. These world-renowned wines can attract ultra-premium price tags, so let's find out a bit more.

Burgundy: Situated in central–eastern France and home to ethereal PINOT NOIR that carefully balances delicate red fruit flavours with savoury undertones. Entry-level wines are labelled as BOURGOGNE and are usually mid-range priced. Next are village wines, which attract higher prices, while the most expensive wines come from vineyards with *premier cru* or *grand cru* status. Famous *grand cru* vineyards include CLOS DE VOUGEOT, CLOS DE TART and ROMANÉE-CONTI. BURGUNDY is famous for terroir-driven wines that are believed to reflect the characteristics of specific vineyard sites.

Bordeaux: Famed for long-lived, powerful yet elegant reds based on CABERNET SAUVIGNON, MERLOT and, to a lesser extent, CABERNET FRANC (and other permitted grapes). BORDEAUX is situated in southwestern France and is split into two parts, the Left Bank with CABERNET SAUVIGNON-dominant blends and the Right Bank with MERLOT-dominant blends. Acclaimed Left Bank appellations include SAINT-ESTÈPHE, PAUILLAC, SAINT-JULIEN and MARGAUX, containing prestigious châteaux vineyards such as Lafite Rothschild, Latour and Margaux. SAINT-ÉMILION and POMEROL are the leading Right Bank appellations, home to some of the most expensive MERLOT-based wines on the globe, such as Château Cheval Blanc and Pétrus.

Barolo: This small and prestigious region in Piedmont, northwestern Italy, produces premium reds made from the NEBBIOLO grape. Wines have traditionally benefited from extended cellaring to soften the mouth-puckering tannins and acidity common in NEBBIOLO from this region. Some producers have experimented with different sites and winemaking techniques to produce more accessible styles that can be enjoyed younger. As with red BURGUNDY, increased attention is now being paid to terroir and the stylistic differences between the 11 villages within BAROLO, such as LA MORRA and SERRALUNGA D'ALBA.

Barossa Valley: This warm, sunny wine region lies about an hour's drive from Adelaide, SOUTH AUSTRALIA. BAROSSA VALLEY'S climate lends itself to producing big and bold red wines, predominantly made from SHIRAZ, that have become the benchmark for full-bodied, rich, oaky and velvety styles made from this grape. Some producers are experimenting with more restrained styles of SHIRAZ, but the opulent style described is the region's signature. Penfolds is a famous producer in the region, with significant plantings here.

Napa Valley: CALIFORNIA'S most prestigious wine region, known for bold and powerful red wines based on the BORDEAUX varieties, principally CABERNET SAUVIGNON. The warmer temperatures here compared to BORDEAUX produce richer reds with a full body and high levels of alcohol. NAPA VALLEY achieved worldwide interest after a blind wine-tasting competition in 1976 – known as the 'Judgement of Paris' – in which the NAPA VALLEY winery Stag's Leap Wine Cellars was rated the most highly by judges, beating BORDEAUX's top red wines. Other famous wineries here include Screaming Eagle, Harlan Estate and Opus One.

IMPRESS FOR LESS:
RED WINES

If you're looking for quality red wine without the hefty price tag, here are some of my favourite regions to explore.

Stellenbosch: South Africa's picturesque and premier wine region situated in the Western Cape is just inland from the cool False Bay, which contributes a freshness to the wines produced here. With the first vines planted over 300 years ago, *STELLENBOSCH* is famed for quality, age-worthy and attractively priced reds based on the Bordeaux varieties *CABERNET SAUVIGNON* and *MERLOT*, which are often made into *BORDEAUX*-style blends. Acclaimed producers in the region include Kanonkop and Meerlust.

Rioja: Situated in central–northern Spain, this is considered one of the world's most famous wine regions. Red *RIOJA* wines, with their approachable yet sophisticated style based on the *TEMPRANILLO* grape, grace restaurant and bar lists across the globe. The most complex and age-worthy are typically labelled as Reserva and Gran Reserva. Consistently admired as one of the world's leading fine red wine regions, *RIOJA* produces particularly well-priced wines in comparison to others. Top producers include López de Heredia, Muga and La Rioja Alta.

Douro Valley: This classic and breathtaking Portuguese wine region is situated on the winding river Douro in northern Portugal. Its iconic vineyards are planted on dramatic terraces either side of the river. Although prices have gradually crept up, the region still offers great value when compared to other fine red regions. Wines are often blends based on the flagship grape *TOURIGA NACIONAL*, with many of the best examples being full-bodied, with black fruit, floral notes and long ageing potential.

Southern Italy: Away from the high prices commanded in Tuscany and Piedmont, there are a number of established and up-and-coming wine regions in the south that offer characterful and well-priced reds. In the volcanic regions of *CAMPANIA* and *BASILICATA* the prized *AGLIANICO* makes complex and structured reds similar to *CABERNET SAUVIGNON* at wallet-friendly prices. *PUGLIA* was once known for bulk wine production, but several producers are now making affordable, good-quality, bold and smooth reds based on *PRIMITIVO* and *NEGROAMARO*. Sicilian wines are in vogue, with talented producers making mineral-driven reds from native varieties.

Languedoc: Hugging the southern coast of France, just south of the *RHÔNE* and adjacent to *PROVENCE*, lies the *LANGUEDOC* wine region. Traditionally known for producing large volumes of simple wines, it has raised its reputation through investment and advances in cultivation and winemaking to the point where the great quality of expressive wines found in this region is now recognized. Reds are typically blends based principally on **GRENACHE, SYRAH, CARIGNAN** and **MOURVÈDRE**, with some excellent full-bodied, powerful and layered examples coming from the appellations of *LA CLAPE, TERRASSES DU LARZAC* and *PIC SAINT-LOUP*.

CLASSIC FINE WHITE AND SPARKLING WINES

Here are five regions producing classic fine white wines and sparkling wine. These well-known wines can be mid-range priced through to ultra-premium, so let's have a closer look.

Champagne: The most significant sparkling wine region in the world is situated in northern France. As of 2023, there are 24 international *CHAMPAGNE* houses known as the Grandes Marques, which include the likes of Billecart-Salmon, Moët & Chandon and Veuve Clicquot, working with a network of growers and their own vineyards across the region to produce their *CHAMPAGNE*. The term 'grower *CHAMPAGNE*' refers to smaller, artisan producers that grow all their own grapes to make their wines. *CHAMPAGNE* gets its distinctive brioche and pastry notes from lees ageing (see page 43). A minimum of 15 months is required for non-vintage styles, while vintage *CHAMPAGNE* is often aged for several years to a decade or longer.

Burgundy: The birthplace of CHARDONNAY and internationally recognized for producing many of the finest expressions of this grape. As with red BURGUNDY, the hierarchy of wines – starting from the larger regional appellation up to single vineyards – is key, and is connected to the nuances of terroir. The finest white BURGUNDY balances subtle fruit, mineral qualities and nuances of wood from French oak barrels, and can be aged for a decade or longer. The most famous *grand cru* vineyard is *LE MONTRACHET*.

Chablis: Situated in the far north of the region, the 'other' CHARDONNAY from BURGUNDY is usually referred to as *CHABLIS* as opposed to white BURGUNDY to highlight its stylistic difference. So how does it differ? First, the more northerly climate gives the wines racy acidity; second, the region's famous Kimmeridgian soils, which date back about 150 million years and contain fossilized seashells, are believed to contribute to the recognizable elegance and mineral quality of the wines; and third, its winemakers generally avoid using new oak barrels to retain the pureness and freshness of the style.

Sancerre: Arguably producing the best examples of SAUVIGNON BLANC in the world, this premium region is situated inland in the *LOIRE*, and is known for dry and elegant white wines, with a petrichor (the scent of rain on parched earth) quality and mouthwatering acidity. Like BURGUNDY, this region is also famous for its soils, which are considered to contribute to the mineral-driven and slightly smoky quality found in SAUVIGNON BLANC here.

Mosel: This scenic region, situated in western Germany, is famed for its steep vineyards grown on the slopes of the winding river Mosel. It's considered to be the country's oldest wine region and is known for prized examples of RIESLING, regarded among the finest in the world. Top examples of *MOSEL* RIESLING are known for their delicate body and flavours, and ability to age for decades, developing honeyed and petrol notes over time. They vary from bone-dry to sweet, with sweeter examples displaying riper fruit and more body. Famous villages include *WEHLEN*, *BERNKASTEL* and *PIESPORT*.

IMPRESS FOR LESS:
WHITE AND SPARKLING WINES

If you're partial to champagne and the fine white wines in the preceding list, but looking for something a bit different that's also kinder on the wallet, here are five delicious alternatives to try.

Spanish Cava: The sparkling wine for those with champagne taste on a prosecco budget! Cava is made in the same way as champagne, but typically sold at markedly lower prices. Production is concentrated in the PENEDÈS region in CATALONIA and the traditional white grapes used are MACABEO, XAREL-LO and PARELLADA (but others are permitted). The rules for production have tightened over the years, improving cava's quality, and today the minimum lees ageing requirement is 9 months for non-vintage styles and 36 months for Cava de Paraje Calificado (which sits at the top of the hierarchy). Cava is food-friendly and can range from light and refreshing to rich and gastronomic in style.

French Aligoté: Aligot-who? It's likely that you haven't come across this other white grape grown in BURGUNDY, which accounts for just over five per cent of plantings in the region. As prices for white BURGUNDY (CHARDONNAY) continue to rise, drinkers have been looking for something similar that's well-priced and hits the spot. Step forward ALIGOTÉ, which is having a well-deserved renaissance. It shares some similarities with CHARDONNAY, having flavours of citrus, orchard fruit and white flowers, and a mineral-fresh quality. Look out for examples produced by top domaines and producers

in the region, which can present incredible value for the quality of winemaker.

Greek Assyrtiko: Widely credited as Greece's answer to CHABLIS, this premium white grape thrives in the volcanic soils of its native SANTORINI. It delivers poised, complex and dry white wines that display bright citrus through to riper tropical fruit flavours that retain refreshing acidity. Prices for SANTORINI ASSYRTIKO have crept up over the years, driven by a number of factors, including tourism on the island, but relatively well-priced options are still available – and you can also find affordable examples from elsewhere in Greece.

Hungarian Furmint: Best known for being a key player in the world-renowned sweet wines of TOKAJ, FURMINT is now also being explored more for its quality dry white wines. If you like the citrus notes and crispness of SANCERRE, then this unique grape, with its energetic pucker, might be the white wine for you. Dry styles can range from light, zesty and easy-drinking to riper and slightly spicy.

Rías Baixas Albariño: Like a dry MOSEL RIESLING, Spain's RÍAS BAIXAS ALBARIÑO offers a vibrant and fresh white with mineral nuances and lip-smacking acidity. This popular and typically well-priced grape tends to be less aromatic and floral than RIESLING, but both can display concentrated citrus and stone fruit flavours. Given ALBARIÑO's depth of flavour and high acidity, producers are increasingly looking to see how the grape ages – so look out for ALBARIÑO with a bit of bottle age in your specialist wine shops and on restaurant lists.

LESSER-KNOWN WINE COUNTRIES

Wine is about experimentation, and these five countries are doing some exciting things with grapes. Put them on your list to try.

England: The English wine industry is dominated by quality, traditional-method sparkling wines. These wines have achieved great success at international wine competitions, often beating champagne in blind tastings. Smaller amounts of still white wine are produced – light to richer styles of CHARDONNAY and zesty and herbaceous BACCHUS – and a little bit of rosé and red wine – both generally light, fresh and fruity in style. Wine production is concentrated in KENT, SUSSEX, HAMPSHIRE and ESSEX.

China: With a range of wines from entry level to premium quality styles, red grapes account for the majority of plantings here, with CABERNET SAUVIGNON leading the other BORDEAUX varieties MERLOT and CABERNET FRANC. There has been investment from French wine powerhouses into the luxury market, such as the launch of LVMH's Ao Yun and Domaines Barons de Rothschild's Long Dai – I've enjoyed some opulent and full-bodied reds. Notable regions include SHANDONG, NINGXIA and YUNNAN.

Canada: Wine production is concentrated in ONTARIO and BRITISH COLUMBIA. These relatively cool wine regions grow a variety of grapes across a diverse landscape with many different terroirs. In ONTARIO the speciality sweet Icewine is produced (see page 217), as well as dry, aromatic whites from grapes

such as RIESLING, and elegant styles of CHARDONNAY, PINOT NOIR and CABERNET FRANC. BRITISH COLUMBIA has some warmer pockets, which enable it to grow MERLOT (and other BORDEAUX varieties) in addition to cooler climate grapes. Make sure the subregion of OKANAGAN VALLEY in BRITISH COLUMBIA is on your radar, as it has an excellent reputation for high-quality wines.

Greece: Viticulture dates back thousands of years here, and today there are many high-quality and interesting wines made from unique indigenous varieties. I'm a fan of the red grape XINOMAVRO, which is regularly compared with the much more expensive wines of BAROLO (NEBBIOLO), while the quality white grape ASSYRTIKO has attractive flavours, elegance and bright acidity.

Romania: This country is producing an eclectic mix of well-priced wines made from both international and local varieties. I've tried some delicious, fruity and accessible PINOT NOIR, priced at a fraction of the cost of those found elsewhere, plus good examples of CABERNET SAUVIGNON, MERLOT and SAUVIGNON BLANC. Keep an eye out for wines made from the native white grape FETEASCĂ REGALĂ, which produces dry, aromatic and crisp wines, and the red grape FETEASCĂ NEAGRĂ, which makes bold red wines with black fruit and savoury nuances.

COOL-CLIMATE NEW WORLD REGIONS

Many of these regions are blessed with sunshine but have cooling influences, leading to wines with vibrant fruit balanced by fresh acidity. Their styles straddle the traditional interpretation of Old World and New World styles, with many producers looking to create wines with restraint and finesse.

Cape South Coast, South Africa: This cool part of the WESTERN CAPE benefits from chilly ocean breezes and cooling influences from areas of high altitude. It's particularly recognized for its fresh and elegant wines made from SAUVIGNON BLANC, CHARDONNAY and PINOT NOIR. Look out for wines from ELGIN and WALKER BAY (which is home to the much-admired Hemel-en-Aarde wards) for some of the best wines in this region.

Victoria, Australia: As with the CAPE SOUTH COAST (above), ocean breezes and altitude make Victoria markedly cooler than many of Australia's other leading regions. Look out for delicious expressions of PINOT NOIR and CHARDONNAY from YARRA VALLEY and MORNINGTON PENINSULA, and peppery SHIRAZ from GEELONG that is typically more NORTHERN RHÔNE than BAROSSA VALLEY in style.

Santa Barbara, California: If you start your journey in warm NAPA VALLEY and head south around 600 km (370 miles) down the famous coastal Route 101, you will hit the cooler region of SANTA BARBARA. There are several commended subregions known for producing refined and complex expressions of SYRAH, PINOT NOIR and CHARDONNAY.

STA RITA HILLS has the highest reputation for BURGUNDIAN styles of CHARDONNAY and PINOT NOIR, and some excellent expressions of SYRAH too.

Willamette Valley, Oregon: Cooler than the neighbouring states of CALIFORNIA and WASHINGTON, this area of Oregon has attracted interest for producing restrained and sophisticated styles of CHARDONNAY and PINOT NOIR. A number of producers from BURGUNDY have established estates here, recognizing the parallels between the two regions. The subregion of DUNDEE HILLS has attracted particular acclaim for top expressions of PINOT NOIR.

Marlborough, New Zealand: Elevated to new heights in the 1980s by the acclaimed producer Cloudy Bay, MARLBOROUGH SAUVIGNON BLANC is one of the world's most loved wines. Situated in the north of New Zealand's South Island, the region benefits from high sunshine and cooling influences. SAUVIGNON BLANC dominates plantings in this region, and the wines are known for bright acidity, zesty citrus notes, tropical fruit and characteristic herbaceous nuances.

CROWD-PLEASERS

If you ever find yourself bewildered by a wine list or wandering hopelessly around the wine aisles, struggling to pick something to suit all palates, then remember these fail-safe options for winning over a crowd.

French crémant: The name given to champagne-method bubbles made in France outside the *CHAMPAGNE* region. Crémants are found in many regions, including the *LOIRE*, *ALSACE*, *BORDEAUX*, *BURGUNDY*, *JURA* and *LIMOUX*. Often brilliantly priced and accessible on the palate too, these are made from a range of grapes, depending on which region they are from. They can have slightly softer-textured bubbles than champagne and fruitier flavours.

Italian white wines: Some people are more sensitive to oaky whites than others, and prefer an easy-drinking style of white with fresh flavours. You can't go wrong with a number of dry, unoaked Italian whites that bring bright citrus and orchard fruit and refreshing quality to the glass. **PINOT GRIGIO** is a reliable option, but how about trying a **VERDICCHIO**, or the wines from *GAVI* (**CORTESE**) and *SOAVE* (**GARGANEGA**)?

Provence-style rosé: Pale, pink and easy on the eye, Provence-style rosés are always a good option for a crowd – a place where white wine drinkers and red wine drinkers can meet in the middle. These wines are usually unoaked, with subtle berry, stone fruit, or melon flavours, and a fresh finish

that makes them enjoyable as a sipping wine and versatile to accompany a range of dishes.

Red Rioja: A safe bet when ordering for a group. In particular, the more youthful Crianza styles are extremely approachable – they typically have a medium body, a nice amount of berry-fruit flavours accompanied by toasty or vanilla notes from oak, and usually nice, smooth tannins. In a group dining situation, they are great with vegetarian, poultry and meat dishes and they can also be served with more robust fish and shellfish dishes, too.

Malbec: Whether you're planning a barbecue or heading out to steak night, **MALBEC** is a dependable red option to go alongside meat platters. Not too light, not too gripping – it tends to produce bold and characterful reds, with juicy fruit and a lovely, approachable velvet texture.

PARTY WINES

I love hosting a drinks party, and making sure my guests have something nice in the glass is a top priority. For a standing set-up with light nibbles, I'll usually look to serve easy-to-love, versatile wines that are suitable to drink with or without food.

Sparkling wines: Fizz creates a celebratory buzz and is refreshing in style – but beware, bubbles always seem to be consumed very quickly. If you're looking to splurge, go for a classic champagne (look out for offers, see page 175), or in the UK, you can usually pick up vintage styles of English sparkling wine for around the same price as non-vintage champagne. For more affordable bubbles, try Spanish cava, French crémant or South African cap classique styles.

Lightly oaked white wines: Lightly oaked CHARDONNAY is my go-to white – something with a bit of texture and fruit, as light, dry, mineral-driven whites can feel a bit acidic after a while. White BURGUNDY does the trick, and for affordable and approachable options, I'll pick something from the MÂCONNAIS. Also consider CHARDONNAY from cool-climate New World wine regions, such as VICTORIA (in Australia) or CASABLANCA (in Chile). But if you know that your friends are truly not CHARDONNAY or oak fans, the Italian white wines on page 214 are good options.

Light- to medium-bodied red wines with medium alcohol: Remember when picking a red for a drinks party not only to consider something that is approachable without food, but also to look at the alcohol content. A couple of glasses of 15% ABV SHIRAZ with a handful of nuts could go straight to your guests' heads. Go for lower alcohol reds – a light South African CINSAULT or a fresh Sicilian FRAPPATO. Styles such as these have low tannins and fruity flavours, so can also be served lightly chilled, making them a refreshing red option for party sipping.

Boxed wines/canned wines: The boxed and canned wine market has come on hugely; no longer are these formats reserved for lower quality wines, but many fantastic producers are choosing to use these more sustainable forms of packaging. Boxed wines are great for a party as they usually hold a couple of bottles of wine, and many contemporary examples have eye-catching artwork and look great perched on the side at an event. Cans can also be kept on ice for guests to help themselves.

Magnums: If you have appropriate chilling facilities to accommodate larger bottles, treat your guests to a double-bottle size. The larger format feels delightfully indulgent – it shows you're ready to party! Consider magnums for dinners too, as they are a real showstopper on the table.

LOWER ALCOHOL WINES

There are many personal, social and health reasons why we might consider buying lower alcohol wines, so let's take a look at five wines that fit the bill.

Vinho Verde: These fresh, zesty and sometimes spritzy Portuguese whites are lower in alcohol (around 8.5–11.5% ABV), so make a great choice for daytime and summer sipping.

Muscadet: This refreshing white comes from the coastal region of the *LOIRE*, and is typically light in body, with citrus and apple flavours and low levels of alcohol (around 11–12% ABV).

German Riesling: Depending on the style, some German RIESLING can be as low as 6 or 7% ABV (but note that the lowest-alcohol examples may be off-dry to sweet).

Moscato d'Asti: This lightly sparkling wine is playful, floral and sweet, and at around 5.5% ABV, is a great low-alcohol dessert-wine option.

Beaujolais: Produced from the red GAMAY grape, fruity *BEAUJOLAIS* wines have traditionally had moderate levels of alcohol. Beware, though, that recent warmer vintages have seen them creep up to 13 or 14% ABV, so make sure to check the label.

SOMETHING DIFFERENT

These five wines offer something a little unusual with which to surprise your guests (in a good way) at home or in a restaurant. More niche wines like these tend to be available at restaurants with broader wine offerings or at specialist wine shops.

Pét-nat: This is the nickname for French petillant-naturel, or 'naturally sparkling', wines. They are made using an ancient method, believed to be the earliest way of creating sparkling wines. It involves only one fermentation – in fact, the wine is bottled and sealed before it completes fermentation, and the carbon dioxide released during this process is trapped in the bottle to create a lightly sparkling wine. Pét-nat tends to have a cloudy appearance, as the used yeast remains in the bottle. These sparklings are fashionable, fun and approachable, and the best examples are fresh and fruity.

Icewine/Eiswein: A speciality style of sweet wine made from frozen grapes that are left on the vine into winter, and then pressed in a way that separates the concentrated juices from the frozen water. These wines have high levels of sugar, with pure and fresh fruit flavours. They are made in Canada (typically from the hybrid grape VIDAL along with RIESLING), and also in Germany and Austria, where they are known as Eiswein. They can be quite tricky to find internationally and are usually quite expensive, but they make a delightful treat for a dessert wine.

Vermouth: This is something I'm really into. Vermouth is commonly made from a simple, low-alcohol wine that is then fortified and infused with herbs, spices, botanicals and fruits. The key styles are bianco (white) or rosso (red), and the flavour varies from dry to sweet. It is used in cocktails, such as a Martini, but some styles are great simply with tonic or soda water, or just over ice.

Txakoli: A white wine from the Basque region of Spain. It's a dry, youthful style of wine, with bright citrus notes, herbal nuances, lip-smacking acidity and a touch of effervescence. In the region, it's traditionally poured from a height to accentuate its light spritz. This easy-drinking and moreish wine makes a charming aperitif with salty snacks.

Vin Jaune: A speciality dry wine made in the alpine region of Jura in eastern France, recognizable for the squat bottle it comes in, called a 'clavelin'. Vin Jaune (literally 'yellow wine') is made from the white grape SAVAGNIN and gets its distinct flavour profile from an extended period of ageing under yeast. This grape can display unique flavours such as dried stone fruit with doughy, nutty and tangy nuances. It is is wonderful with rich poultry dishes and strong cheese.

Index

spicy food 118
Stellenbosch 206
stoppers 186
storing wine 188-9
structured wine 26
sugar content 22, 24, 26
sulphites 45
sulphur dioxide 45
sweet foods 116, 152-5
sweet wines 22, 65, 182, 184, 217
sweetness (wine) 26, 29, 63
swirling 12-13
syrah 14, 94
slow roast lamb paired with syrah 130

T
tannin 22, 24, 25, 29
tapas and sherry 122
tartrates 17
taste 13, 20-1 *see also* wine tasting
temperature, serving 184-5
tempranillo 100
terroir 39
texture (food) 116
texture (wine) 22, 24
Thai cuisine 164-5
tofu 141
tomatoes 140-1
touch 13, 24-6, 29 *see also* mouthfeel
truffles 140-1
turkey 125
Tuscany 104
Txakoli 217

U
umami flavours (food) 118
USA 70, 72, 74, 82, 88, 90, 92, 94, 213

V
vacuum pumps 186
varietal wines 42
vegan wines 141
vegetables 140-1, 142
vegetarian & vegan food 140-1
Vermouth 217
vessels 21, 34, 42
Victoria, Australia 213

vieilles vignes 35
Vietnamese cuisine 165
Vin Jaune 217
Vin Méthode Nature 45
vines, growing
  geographical areas 36-7
  influence of place 38-9
  mature vines 35
  terroir 39
Vinho Verde 216
vintage 39, 56, 63, 168
viognier 25, 82

W
weather 39
white wines 53, 180, 183, 184
  classic 208-9
  recommended 210-11, 214, 215
Willamette Valley, Oregon 213
wine
  buying 173-5
  geographical areas 36-7
  influence of place 38-9
  manufacture 40-7
  opening 177-9
  recommended 206-7, 210-11, 214-17
wine closures 176-9
wine labels, reading 168-72
wine lists 198-201
wine regions 168, 169, 170, 172, 174
  red wines 204-7
  sparkling wines 208-11
  white wines 208-11
wine styles 14
wine tasting 12-13, 23, 28-9
  aroma and flavour wheel 20-1
  notes 30-1
  sight/appearance 12, 14-17, 28
  smell & taste 18-23, 28-9
  sound 27, 29
  subjectivity of 11
  touch 13, 24-6, 29

Acknowledgements

First and foremost, to my friend, creative partner and photographer for this book, Laura Jalbert, thank you for bringing this project to life, for believing in me and for making every work venture we do infinitely enjoyable.

A special thank you to Georgi Davenport, Sean Evans, Matt Mawtus, the Hamills, Elizabeth Pearson, Ilaria Verde and Emma Young for their time and brilliant advice on this project. And to my family, in particular my husband G, for your unwavering love, support and counsel, and for all those magical wine experiences over the years. To my brother Alex for that initial brainstorming session where we came up with the name *Taste, Pair, Pour* and talked about a wine book full of life and colour.

It was such a privilege to speak with so many accomplished chefs, food experts and local sources who shared their knowledge and provided colour in the 'Flavours from around the World' section of this book – thank you, Dipna Anand, Isidoro Hamui Hanono, Eddie Lim, Yui Miles, Max Redmond Roche, Ilaria Verde and Lucía Acevedo.

What a pleasure it has been to work with the team at Octopus – Alison, Juliette, Alex, Ellen, Katherine – thank you for giving me so much creative freedom and for making this whole project so very exciting from the start. Thank you to our illustrator Kiki, for bringing such character and imagination to the illustrations throughout this book. And to our fab food stylists Natalie Thomson and Caitlin Nuala – what fun we had.

And thank you to everyone I've shared a glass with over the years! All those moments and memories built the foundations for this book.

The photo shoots were made possible by a number of wonderful partners. Thank you, Riedel, for providing your beautiful wine glasses used throughout the book – and to HIDE Restaurant for the gorgeous location.

A huge thank you to the many wineries, agencies and PRs who supported the shoots:

Agricola Querciabella, Alex Foillard, Badenhorst Family Wines, Billecart-Salmon, Black Stallion, Bodega Catena Zapata, CVNE, Château de Valois, Château Léoube, Château Suduiraut, De Haan Altés, Domaine de la Noblaie, Domaine la Haute Févrie, Domaine François Merlin, Elena Walch, Famille Bourgeois, Giant Steps, Giacomo Fenocchio, González Byass, Joh. Jos. Prüm, Joseph Drouhin, La Rioja Alta SA, Le Clos du Caillou, Louis Jadot, Penfolds, Paul Jaboulet Aîné, Quinta do Noval, Weingut Bründlmayer.

Armit Wines, Bancroft Wines, Clementine Communications, Dillon Morrall, EightyFour PR, Emma Wellings PR, Fiona Campbell, Hue & Cry Agency, Majorly PR, Pol Roger Portfolio, R&R, Smith & Vine, Swig, The Wine Society.

Picture Credits

35 Hannah Milnes; 69 Eckhard Supp/Alamy Stock Photo; 198 Lisa Linder/4Corners

About the Author

Charlotte Kristensen is a wine columnist, communicator and educator based in London. Prior to focusing on wine, she worked as a lawyer in the City of London. After falling in love with the world of wine while living in New York, Charlotte decided to leave the corporate world and made the leap into wine. In 2018, she set up her Instagram account @thelondonwinegirl to record her journey, and now has followers around the world. Charlotte completed the prestigious Diploma in Wines with the Wine and Spirits Education Trust (WSET) in 2020 and is a certified WSET wine educator. In 2022 she became the weekly wine columnist for *You* magazine at the *Mail on Sunday*. Charlotte runs supper clubs, tastings and events, and works with wine regions and brands from around the world.

@ @thelondonwinegirl